GREENLIGHTS

GREENLIGHTS

Matthew
McConaughey

HEADLINE

First published in 2020 by
HEADLINE PUBLISHING GROUP
First published in the US in 2020 by Crown,
an imprint of Random House, a division of
Penguin Random House LLC, New York.
First published in paperback in 2023 by
HEADLINE PUBLISHING GROUP

1

Cataloguing in Publication Data is available from the
British Library
Photo on page 269 by Anne Marie Fox.
Photo on page 109 courtesy of
Universal Studios Licensing LLC.
Photo on page 142 licensed by:
Warner Bros. Entertainment.
All rights reserved.
All other photos are courtesy of the author.

ISBN: 978 1 4722 8087 9

Offset in 11.9/15.14 pt WilliamsCaslonText
by Jouve (UK), Milton Keynes

Printed and bound in Great Britain by Clays Ltd, Elcograf S.p.A.
Book design by Ian Dingman

Headline's policy is to use papers that are natural,
renewable and recyclable products and made from
wood grown in well-managed forests and other controlled
sources. The logging and manufacturing processes
are expected to conform to the environmental
regulations of the country of origin.

HEADLINE PUBLISHING GROUP
An Hachette UK Company
Carmelite House
50 Victoria Embankment
London
EC4Y 0DZ

www.headline.co.uk
www.hachette.co.uk

To the only thing I ever knew
I wanted to be, and family

Contents

greenlights

1-22-89

I'VE FOUND MYSELF

- the most difficult word in the universe?

- <u>WHOWHATWHEREWHENHOW</u>?? — and that's the truth
  <u>WHY</u>? — is even bigger

. I think I'll write a book. ——————
             word
A ~~book~~ about my life.
I wonder who would give a damn
~~About~~ the pleasures and the strife?

————— I think I'll write a book. —————
~~to~~ Help the generations with the truth about
the past? Who's to say, one would agree?
Shit!, I'm tired. Hope that these thoughts last. . .

————— I still think I'll write a book. —————

- mood for the saying
- favorite one
- phycological
- let life be - no - the we are cowards
- ... a book. .

March 11

THIS IS NOT A TRADITIONAL memoir. Yes, I tell stories from the past, but I have no interest in nostalgia, sentimentality, or the retirement most memoirs require. This is not an advice book, either. Although I like preachers, I'm not here to preach and tell you what to do.

This is an approach book. I am here to share stories, insights, and philosophies that can be objectively understood, and if you choose, subjectively adopted, by either changing your reality, or changing how you see it.

This is a playbook, based on adventures in my life. Adventures that have been significant, enlightening, and funny, sometimes because they were meant to be but mostly because they didn't try to be. I'm an optimist by nature, and humor has been one of my great teachers. It has helped me deal with pain, loss, and lack of trust. I'm not perfect; no, I step in shit all the time and recognize it when I do. I've just learned how to scrape it off my boots and carry on.

We all step in shit from time to time. We hit roadblocks, we fuck up, we get fucked, we get sick, we don't get what we want, we cross thousands of "could have done better"s and "wish that wouldn't have happened"s in life. Stepping in shit is inevitable, so let's either see it as good luck, or figure out how to do it less often.

To Life

I'VE BEEN IN THIS LIFE for fifty years, trying to work out its riddle for forty-two, and keeping diaries of clues to that riddle for the last thirty-five. Notes about successes and failures, joys and sorrows, things that made me marvel, and things that made me laugh out loud. Thirty-five years of realizing, remembering, recognizing, gathering, and jotting down what has moved me or turned me on along the way. How to be fair. How to have less stress. How to have fun. How to hurt people less. How to get hurt less. How to be a good man. How to get what I want. How to have meaning in life. How to be more me.

I never wrote things down to remember; I always wrote things down so I could forget. The idea of revisiting my life and musings was a daunting one; I wasn't sure if I'd enjoy the company. Recently, I worked up the courage to sit down with those diaries and have a look at the thirty-five years of writing about who I've been over the last fifty. And you know what? I enjoyed myself more than I thought I would. I laughed, I cried, I realized I had remembered more than I expected, and forgot less.

What did I find? I found stories I witnessed and experienced, lessons I learned and forgot, poems, prayers, prescriptions, answers to questions I had, reminders of questions I still have, affirmations for certain doubts, beliefs about what matters, theories on relativity, and a whole bunch of bumperstickers.* I found consistent ways that I approached life that gave me more satisfaction, at the time, and still.

I found a reliable theme.

So, I packed up those journals and took a one-way ticket to solitary confinement in the desert, where I began writing what you hold now: an album, a record, a story of my life so far.

Things I witnessed, dreamed, chased, gave and received.

Truth bombs that interrupted my space and time in ways I could not ignore.

Contracts I have made with myself, many of which I live up to, most of which I still pursue.

These are my sights and seens, felts and figured outs, cools and shamefuls.

Graces, truths, and beauties of brutality.

Initiations, invitations, calibrations, and graduations.

Getting away withs, getting caughts, and getting wets trying to dance between the raindrops.

Rites of passage.

All between or on the other sides of persistence and letting go, on the way to the science of satisfaction in this great experiment called life.

---

* I've always loved bumper stickers, so much so that I've stuck *bumper* to *sticker* and made them one word, *bumpersticker*. They're lyrics, one-liners, quick hitters, unobtrusive personal preferences that people publicly express. They're cheap and they're fun. They don't have to be politically correct because, well, they're just bumperstickers. From the font they're in, to the color scheme, to the word or words they say, a bumpersticker tells you a lot about the person behind the wheel in front of you. Their political views, if they've got a family or not, if they're free spirits or conformists, funny or serious, what kind of pets they have, what kind of music they like, even what their religious beliefs might be. Over the last fifty years I've been collecting my bumperstickers. Some I've seen, some I've heard, some I stole, some I dreamed, some I said. Some are funny, some are serious, but they all stuck with me . . . because that's what bumperstickers do. I've included some of my favorites in this book.

Hopefully, it's medicine that tastes good, a couple of aspirin instead of the infirmary, a spaceship to Mars without needing your pilot's license, going to church without having to be born again, and laughing through the tears.

It's a love letter.

To life.

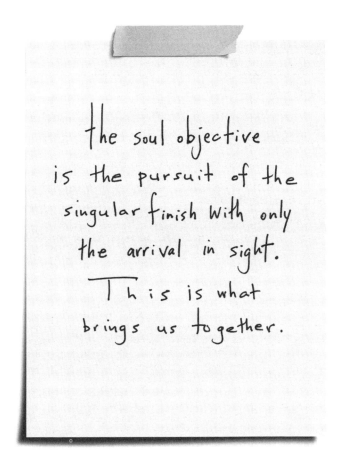

the soul objective
is the pursuit of the
singular finish with only
the arrival in sight.
This is what
brings us together.

Sometimes you gotta go back to go forward. And i don't mean goin back to reminisce or chase ghosts. I mean go back to see where you came from, where you been, how you got HERE.

— mdm
Lincoln Ad, 2014

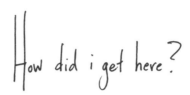

How did i get here?

I'VE EARNED A FEW SCARS getting through this rodeo of humanity. I've been good at it, I've been not so good at it, and ultimately, I've found some pleasure in all of it, either way. Here are some facts about me to help set the table.

I am the youngest brother of three and the son of parents who were twice divorced and thrice married, to each other.

We grew up saying "I love you" to each other. We meant it.

I got whipped until my butt bled for putting on a Cracker Jack tattoo when I was ten.

When I first threatened to run away from home, my parents packed my bags for me.

My dad wasn't there the day I was born. He called my mom and said, "Only thing I have to say is if it's a boy, don't name him 'Kelly.'"

The only thing I ever knew I wanted to be was a father.

I learned to swim when my mom threw me in the Llano River and I was either going to float off the rocky waterfall thirty yards downstream or make it to the bank. I made it to the bank.

I was always the first one to wear out the knees in my Toughskin jeans.

For two years I led the Under-12 soccer league in red cards, as a goalie.

When I kept whining about my lone pair of tennis shoes being old and out of fashion, my mom told me, "Keep griping and I'll take you to meet the boy with no feet!!"

I was blackmailed into having sex for the first time when I was fifteen. I was certain I was going to hell for the premarital sex. Today, I am merely certain that I *hope* that's not the case.

I was molested by a man when I was eighteen while knocked unconscious in the back of a van.

I've done peyote in Real de Catorce, Mexico, in a cage with a mountain lion.

I've had seventy-eight stitches sewn into my forehead, by a veterinarian.

I've had four concussions from falling out of four trees, three of them on a full moon.

I've bongoed naked until the cops arrested me.

I resisted arrest.

I applied to Duke, UT Austin, Southern Methodist, and Grambling for my college education. I got accepted to three out of the four.

I've never felt like a victim.

I have a lot of proof that the world is conspiring to make me happy.

I've always gotten away with more in life than in my dreams.

I've had many people give me poems that I did not know I wrote.

I've been naïve, evil, and a cynic. But I am most fearless in my belief of my and mankind's benevolence and the common denominator of values among us.

I believe the truth is only offensive when we're lying.

I was raised on existential outlaw logic, a carnation of malaprops, full of fictitious physics, because if it wasn't true, it ought to be.

There was nothing fictitious about the love, though. The love was real. Bloody sometimes, but never in question.

I learned early on how to get **relative**: how to deal.

I learned resilience, consequences, responsibility, and how to work hard. I learned how to love, laugh, forgive, forget, play, and pray. I learned how to hustle, sell, charm, turn a tide, make a downfall my upfall, and spin a yarn. I learned how to navigate highs and lows, hugs and blows, assets and deficits, love songs and epithets. Especially when faced with the **inevitable.**

This is a story about getting relative with the inevitable.

This is a story about greenlights.

```
The arrival is inevitable: Death.
A unanimous end, a unified destination.
A noun without regard. Our eulogy. Written.
Lived.
The approach is relative: Life.
A singular procession, our personal journey.
A verb with regard. Our résumé. Write it.
Live it.
```

This is the first fifty years of my life, of my résumé so far on the way to my eulogy.

What's a greenlight?

GREENLIGHTS MEAN GO—ADVANCE, CARRY ON, continue. On the road, they are set up to give the flow of traffic the right of way, and when scheduled properly, more vehicles catch more greenlights in succession. **They say proceed.**

In our lives, they are an affirmation of *our* way. They're approvals, support, praise, gifts, gas on our fire, attaboys, and appetites. They're cash money, birth, springtime, health, success, joy, sustainability, innocence, and fresh starts. We love greenlights. They don't interfere with our direction. They're easy. They're a shoeless summer. They say **yes** and give us what we **want.**

Greenlights can also be disguised as yellow and red lights. A caution, a detour, a thoughtful pause, an interruption, a disagreement, indigestion, sickness, and pain. A full stop, a jackknife, an intervention, failure, suffering, a slap in the face, death. We don't like yellow and red lights. They slow us down or stop our flow. They're hard. They're a shoeless winter. They say **no**, but sometimes give us what we **need.**

Catching greenlights is about **skill**: intent, context, consideration, endurance, anticipation, resilience, speed, and discipline. We can catch more greenlights by simply identifying where the red lights are in our life, and then change course to hit fewer of them. We can also earn greenlights, engineer and design for them. We can create more and schedule them in our future—a path of least resistance—through force of will, hard work, and the choices we make. We can be **responsible** for greenlights.

Catching greenlights is also about **timing**. The world's timing, and ours. When we are in the zone, on the frequency, and with the flow. We can catch greenlights by sheer luck, because we are in the right place at the right time. Catching more of them in our future can be about intuition, karma, and fortune. Sometimes catching greenlights is about **fate**.

Navigating the autobahn of life in the best way possible is about getting **relative** with the **inevitable** at the right time. The inevitability of a situation is not relative; *when* we accept the outcome *of* a given situation as inevitable, then *how* we choose to deal with it *is* relative. We either **persist** and continue in our present pursuit of a desired result, **pivot** and take a new tack to get it, or **concede** altogether and tally one up for fate. We push on, call an audible, or wave the white flag and live to fight another day.

The secret to our satisfaction lies in *which* one of these we choose to do *when*.

This is the art of livin.

I believe everything we do in life is part of a plan. Sometimes the plan goes as intended, and sometimes it doesn't. *That's* part of the plan. Realizing *this* is a greenlight in itself.

The problems we face today eventually turn into blessings in the rearview mirror of life. In time, yesterday's red light leads us to a greenlight. All destruction eventually leads to construction, all death eventually leads to birth, all pain eventually leads to pleasure. In this life or the next, what goes down will come up.

It's a matter of how we see the challenge in front of us and how we engage with it. **Persist, pivot, or concede. It's up to us, our choice every time.**

This is a book about how to catch more yeses in a world of nos and how to recognize *when* a no might actually be a yes. This is a book about catching greenlights and realizing that the yellows and reds eventually turn green.

GREENLIGHTS.

By design and on purpose . . . Good luck.

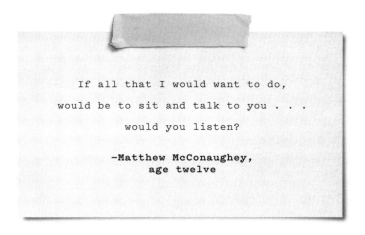

```
     If all that I would want to do,
   would be to sit and talk to you . . .
          would you listen?

          -Matthew McConaughey,
                 age twelve
```

OUTLAW
LOGIC

A WEDNESDAY NIGHT, 1974

DAD HAD JUST GOTTEN HOME from work. Greasy blue button-down with "Jim" on the left chest patch already thrown in the washer, he sat at the head of the table in his sleeveless undershirt. He was hungry. My brothers and I had eaten already and Mom pulled his reheated plate from the oven and shoved it in front of him.

"More potatoes, honey," he said as he dug in.

My dad was a big man. Six foot four, 265 pounds, his "fightin weight," he'd say, "Any lighter I catch a cold." At forty-four years old, those 265 pounds were hanging in places that, at this Wednesday evening dinner, my mom didn't fancy.

"Sure you want more potatoes, FAT MAN?" she barked.

I was crouching behind the couch in the living room, starting to get nervous.

But Dad, head down, quietly continued to eat.

"Look at ya, that fat belly of yours. Sure, eat up, FAT MAN," she yapped as she scraped overwhelming amounts of mashed potatoes onto his plate.

19

That was it. BOOM! Dad flipped the dining table into the ceiling, got up, and began to stalk Mom. "Goddamnit, Katy, I work my ass off all day, I come home, I just want to eat a hot meal in peace."

It was on. My brothers knew the deal, I knew the deal. Mom knew the deal as she ran to the wall-mounted telephone on the other side of the kitchen to call 911.

"You can't leave well enough alone, can ya, Katy?" my dad grumbled through gritted teeth, his forefinger raised at her as he closed in across the kitchen floor.

As he closed in, Mom grabbed the handheld end of the phone off the wall mount and raked it across his brow.

Dad's nose was broken, blood was everywhere.

Mom ran to a cabinet and pulled out a twelve-inch chef's knife, then squared off at him. "C'mon, FAT MAN! I'll cut you from your nuts to your gulliver!"

They circled each other in the middle of the kitchen, Mom waving the twelve-inch blade, Dad with his bloody broken nose and snarling incisors. He grabbed a half-full fourteen-ounce bottle of Heinz ketchup off the counter, unscrewed the cap, and brandished it like her blade.

"C'mon, FAT MAN!" Mom dared him again. "I'll cut you WIIIIDE open!"

Assuming the stance of a mocking matador, Dad began to fling ketchup from the open bottle across Mom's face and body. "Touché," he said, as he pranced right to left.

The more he flipped ketchup on her and dodged her slashing chef's knife, the more frustrated Mom got.

"Touché again!" Dad teased as he splattered a new red stripe across her while eluding another attack.

Around and around they went, until finally, Mom's frustration turned to fatigue. Now covered in ketchup, she dropped the knife on the floor, stood straight, and began to wipe her tears and catch her breath.

Dad dropped the bottle of Heinz, relaxed out of his matador pose, and wiped the blood dripping from his nose with his forearm.

Still facing off, weapons down, they stared at each other for a moment, Mom thumbing the ketchup from her wet eyes, Dad just standing there letting the blood drip from his nose down his chest. Seconds later, they moved toward each other and met in an animal embrace. They dropped to their knees, then to the bloody, ketchup-covered linoleum kitchen floor . . . and made love. A red light turned green.

This is how my parents communicated.

This is why Mom handed Dad an invite to their own wedding and said, "You got twenty-four hours to decide, lemme know."

This is why my mom and dad were married three times and divorced twice—to each other.

This is why my dad broke Mom's middle finger to get it out of his face four separate times.

This is *how* my mom and dad loved each other.

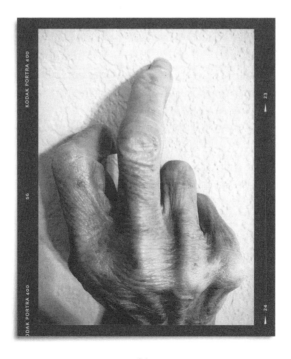

```
the golden rule and
everything in moderation

Two adages, often solicited as
general rules for life.

There's a loophole in each.

Sometimes people don't want to do
what you want to do.

And one man's appetite is another's
indigestion.
```

The McConaughey clan migrated from Ireland to Liverpool, England, to Little Rock, West Virginia, and New Orleans. There is no royalty in our past. There is, however, a lot of cattle thieving, riverboat gambling, and an Al Capone bodyguard.

Dad is from Patterson, Mississippi, but grew up and felt most at home in Morgan City, Louisiana.

Mom's from Altoona, Pennsylvania, but always said she was from Trenton, New Jersey, because "who'd wanna be from a place called Altoona?"

I have two brothers. The oldest, Michael, has been going by "Rooster" for forty years now because even if he goes to sleep at 4:00 A.M. he always wakes at sunrise. When he turned ten, he wanted a little brother for his birthday present, so Mom and Dad adopted my brother Pat from the Methodist home in Dallas, in 1963. Every year Mom and Dad offered to take Pat to meet his birth parents. He declined until he turned nineteen and took them up on their offer.

Mom and Dad arranged the meeting and the three of them drove to the home of Pat's birth parents in Dallas. Parked curbside, Mom and Dad waited in the car while Pat rang the doorbell and went inside. Two minutes later Pat walked out of their house and jumped into the back seat.

"What happened?" they asked him.

"I just wanted to see if my dad was bald cus my hair's thinning."

First marriage
12·22·54

Second marriage
12·18·59

Me, I was an accident. Mom and Dad had been trying to make a baby for years to no avail, so Mom thought I was a tumor until the fifth month of pregnancy. Dad went to the bar instead of the hospital the day I was born, because he suspected I wasn't his anyway.

But I was.

I got my first ass whupping for answering to "Matt" on the kindergarten playground ("You weren't named after a doormat!" Mom screamed), my second for saying "I hate you" to my brother, my third for saying "I can't," and my fourth for telling a lie about a stolen pizza.

I got my mouth washed out with soap for saying "shit," "damn," and "fuck," but I only ever got in real trouble for the using or doing of the words that could harm me. **Words that hurt.** The words that helped engineer who I am because they were more than just words; they were expectations and consequences. They were **values.**

My parents taught me that I was named my name for a reason.

They taught me not to hate.

To never say I can't.

To never lie.

GREENLIGHT.

Words are momentary
intent is momentous

My parents didn't *hope* we would follow their rules, they *expected* us to. A denied expectation hurts more than a denied hope, while a fulfilled hope makes us happier than a fulfilled expectation. Hope's got a higher return on happiness and less debit on denial, it's just not as measurable. My parents measured.

And while I am not advocating for physical punishment as a consequence, I do know that there are a lot of things I didn't do as a kid that I shouldn't have done, because I didn't want to get my ass whupped. I also know that I *did* a lot of things as a kid that I *should* have done, because I wanted my parents' praise and adulation. Consequences, they work both ways.

I come from a loving family. We may not have always liked each other, but we always loved each other. We hug and kiss and wrestle and fight. We don't hold a grudge.

I come from a long line of rule breakers. Outlaw libertarians who vote red down the line because they believe *it'll keep fewer outlaws from trespassin on their territory.*

I come from a family of disciplinarians where you better follow the rules, until you're *man enough to break em.* Where you did what Mom and Dad said "because I said so," and if you didn't, you didn't get grounded, you got the belt or a backhand "because it gets your attention quicker and doesn't take away your most precious resource, time." I come from a family who took you across town to your favorite cheeseburger-and-milkshake joint to celebrate your lesson learned immediately following your corporal correction. I come from a family that might penalize you for breaking the rules, but definitely punished you for getting caught. Slightly calloused on the surface, we know that what tickles us often bruises others— because we deal with or deny it, we're the last to cry uncle to bad luck.

It's a philosophy that has made me a hustler in both senses of the word. I work hard and I like to grift. It's a philosophy that's also led to some great stories.

Like a good southern boy should, I'll start with my mom. She's a true baller, living proof that the value of denial depends on one's level of commitment to it. She's beat two types of cancer on nothing more than aspirin and denial. She's a woman that says "I'm gonna" before she can, "I would" before she could, and "I'll be there" before she's invited. Fiercely loyal to convenience and controversy, she's always had an adversarial relationship with context and consideration, because they ask permission. She might not be the smartest person in the room but she ain't crying.

She's eighty-eight now, and seldom do I go to bed *after* her or wake up *before* her. Her curfew when she was growing up was when she danced holes big enough in the feet of her pantyhose that they came up around her ankles.

Nobody forgives themselves quicker than she does and therefore she carries zero stress. I once asked her if she ever went to bed with any regrets. She quickly told me, "Every night, son. I just forget em by the time I wake up." She always told us, "Don't walk into a place like you wanna buy it, walk in like you own it." Obviously, her favorite word in the English language is *yes*.

In 1977, Mom entered me in the "Little Mr. Texas" contest in Bandera, Texas.

I won a big trophy.

My mom framed this picture and put it on the kitchen wall.

Every morning when I came to breakfast she'd gesture to it and say, "Look at you, winner, Little Mr. Texas, 1977."

Last year I came across the picture in her scrapbook when something caught my eye. Curious, I zoomed in on the nameplate on the trophy. It said "Runner-Up."

I called the queen of relativity, my mom, and said, "Mom, all my life you told me that I was Little Mr. Texas but I was really runner-up?" And she said, "No, the kid who won it, his family had a lot more money than us and they bought him a fancy three-piece suit for the contest. We call that cheatin. No, *you're* Little Mr. Texas."

Then, in 1982, I entered the seventh-grade poetry contest. The night before the deadline, I showed my poem to Mom.

"Not bad, keep working," she said.

I headed back to my room to work on the next draft.

A couple hours later, happy with my progress, I took my poem to Mom again.

She read it. Said nothing.

"Well, what do you think?" I asked

She didn't answer. Instead she opened up a hardcover book to a premarked page, put it in front of me, pointed, and said, "What do *you* think of *that*?"

```
     "if all that I would want to do,
   would be to sit and talk to you . . .
           would you listen?"
```

It was from a poem by Ann Ashford.

"I like it," I said. "Why?"

"Then write *that*," Mom said.

"Write *this*? What do you mean?"

"Do you understand it?"

"Yes, but . . ."

"If you like it and you understand it, then it's *yours*."

"But it's not really mine, Mom, it's Ann Ashford's."

"Does it mean anything to you?"

"Yeah, it's like when someone you love just wants to sit and talk with you."

"Exactly. So if you like it, and you understand it, and it means something to you, it's yours . . . write that."

"And sign my name to it?"

Yes.

I did.

And I won the seventh-grade poetry contest.

My mom had no upbringing, and since she didn't like her life growing up, to survive, she denied it and constructed her own. She's always believed that if you understand something, then you own it, you can sign your name to it, take credit for it, live by it, sell it, and win medals for it. Plagiarism? "Shit, they'll probably never find out and if they do all they can do is blame you and take your medal back, so fuck em," she says.

Obviously my mom was prepping me to be an actor long before it became my vocation.

Knowin the truth, seein the truth, and tellin the truth,

are all different experiences.

While Mom taught us audacious existentialism, Dad taught us common sense. He was a man who valued sirs and ma'ams, discipline, loyalty, persistence, work ethic, humility, rites of passage, respect of women, and making enough money to secure your family. He also painted; took ballet; played for the Green Bay Packers; loved to roll the dice, chase Ponzi schemes, win something instead of buying it; and dreamed of opening a gumbo shack on the beach in Florida if he could ever "hit a lick" big enough to retire.

Deconstructing to *construct* his three sons, Dad respected yellow lights, and he made sure we learned the fundamentals before we expressed our individualism. To use a football term, he taught us to *block and tackle before we could play wideout.*

It was clear who the man of the house was and if any of his three boys wanted to challenge that notion, "You know where to find me," he'd say. We feared him. Not because he ever hurt or abused us but because he was our father. We looked up to him. He was above the law *and* government, and he didn't suffer fools, unless you admitted to

Jim McConaughey

Already a veteran of two Bowl games, big Jim Mc-
Conaughey wants to wind up his collegiate career by
playing in just one more New Year's Day classic . . . A
210-pound, six-foot, two-inch senior end from Metairie,
La., the 22-year-old youngster was a defensive starter
on Bear Bryant's Kentucky club which lost to Santa
Clara in the 1949 Orange Bowl

JIM McCONAUGHEY

. . . Picks last season's Salad
Bowl game and the Texas Tech
struggle as his most-enjoyable
experiences in football. "Our defense was working good in both
of 'em," he grins . . . Jim started
his athletic career at Metairie,
played all sports there and was
member of a nine-man track
team which won the Louisiana
state championship in 1947. He
placed first in the low hurdles,
second in high jump, joined with
three other team mates to get seconds in the 880 and
440-yard relays and the football shuttle . . . He was a
basketball center his sophomore and junior years, then
"got too heavy for all those sports" . . .

He went to Kentucky in 1948, where he was a freshman teammate of Babe Parilli . . . Jim married the
beauty queen of Kentucky's freshman class of '49, making the lovely Kay his bride last Dec. 22 . . . "The Salad
Bowl game was our wedding trip," he grinned . . .

A good dancer who likes "slow music," Jim says he
"doesn't have time" for other hobbies or sports. But he
does play an awful lot of defensive end for the Big Red
and, due to his size, weight, experience and maneuver-
ability, coaches are planning on using "The Bear" on
offense, too, this trip.

His Number Is 88!

being one. A bear of a man with a soft spot for the underdog and the
helpless, he had a rowdy wit about the world and himself. "I'd rather
lose money havin fun than make money being bored," he'd say. He was
also a proud man, and if you gave him a second chance, he'd never forget it. One time in the late '80s, after a banker declined a loan to bail
him out of debt, he said, "Now you can shut that door on me or we can
walk through it together." He got the loan and they walked through it.
He loved to host a party, drink beer, and tell stories, and he was a hand
at all three.

His eldest son was Mike. He had more to do with raising Mike than Pat or me because one, Mike was his first, and two, Dad had to work from the road more often later in life. Mike was a confident, scrappy, hardworking, savvy guy, with a hippie heart full of compassion for the runts of the world. Cool under pressure, with the pain threshold of a badger, he's the first person you'd want with you when the going got tough. "He's survived so many near deaths," Mom always said about him. "You and Pat need prayin for, with Mike it don't matter."

Raised on a reverence for the Old Testament, we were a religious family, but it wasn't *all* fire and brimstone. No, the more merciful teachings of Jesus also had their place in our parents' principles.

When Mike was in high school, he started to grow long hair. It grew long enough that the coach of his football team, Jim Caldwell, asked him to get it cut. My dad agreed, but Mike refused.

Driving Mike to school the next day, my dad said, "You look like a hippie, son, and if you don't cut your *hair,* Coach's gonna cut *you* from the team."

"I don't care, Pop, it's my hair and if he wants to cut me from the team, then he can cut me, I'm not cutting my hair."

"Now, son, listen to me now, quit being stubborn and just cut your damn hair."

Indignant, Mike said, "No sir, Dad. I'm not doing it."

"Son, I'm tellin you—"

"Well, Jesus had long hair too!" Mike blurted.

Quiet. Playing the religious card was a crafty move and Mike knew it might have sealed the deal in his favor. Dad, in silence, just continued to drive.

Just as they were about to arrive at the school entrance, Mike believing his "Jesus" tactic had worked, Dad hit the gas and sped by.

"What the hell, Dad, what are you doin?" Mike asked.

Dad proceeded to drive eight miles past Mike's school, not saying a word. Suddenly he pulled off to the side of the road, leaned over and opened the passenger door, pushed my brother out the door, and said, "Yeah, well, Jesus walked everywhere, too, boy!"

My brother was late for school that day. Not only because my dad dropped him off eight miles from it, but because he stopped by the barbershop on his way there.

Dad had worked his way up from a Texaco gas station manager, to pipe hauler, to pipe salesman in a local company called Gensco. He was a damn *good* pipe salesman. He got Mike a job selling pipe at Gensco as well. My brother became a *great* pipe salesman, and quickly. In less than a year, at twenty-two years of age, Mike was the top salesman in the company. The boss put him on their biggest account: a buyer named Don Knowles. Dad was truly proud of Mike, but Mike was still his son.

We had an old wooden barn in the back of our house by the dirt alleyway where Dad kept an unloaded eighteen-wheeler from his pipe-hauling days. It was a Saturday night.

"Let's drink some beer and throw knives in the barn tonight, son," Dad told Mike.

"Sure, Pop, see you there around sundown."

Around ten o'clock, and after quite a few beers, Dad finally bellied up, "Let's go roll some pipe like we used to, son, it's been a while."

"Rollin pipe" is when you take an unloaded eighteen-wheeler to someone else's pipe yard, load *their* pipe on it, drive away, and steal it. Dad and Mike used to do it on certain Saturday nights back when Dad was hauling.

"Whose pipe you wanna roll, Pop?"

Dad squared off at Mike and said, "Don Knowles."

Oh shit.

"Nah, Dad, I'm not doin that. I just got Don Knowles's account, you know that."

"I do know that. I *got* you that job at Gensco, boy; you wouldn't have that account if it wasn't for me. Where's your loyalty lie, son? With your old man or Don fuckin Knowles?!"

"Now, Dad, you know that ain't fair."

"What ain't fair, boy?! You too good now to roll pipe with your old man like we used to? Huh? You too big-time now, boy?!"

Oh shit.

"Now, Dad, easy . . ."

Dad took off his shirt. "No, let's see how big-time you are now, boy. You think you're man enough not to listen to your old man? You gonna have to whup him to prove it."

"Now, Dad, I don't wanna—"

Whop! Dad walloped an open-palmed right hand across Mike's face. Mike stumbled a step back, then straightened up and started rolling up his sleeves.

"So this is how it's gonna be?" Mike said.

"Yep, this is how it's gonna be, c'mon, boy."

Dad was six four, 265 pounds. Mike was five ten, 180.

Oh shit.

Dad, now crouched, stepped in with a right hook across Mike's jaw. Mike went down. Dad stalked toward him.

On the ground, gathering himself, Mike saw a five-foot 2 x 4 lying on the ground next to him.

Just as Dad came in for another blow, Mike grabbed that 2 x 4 and baseball-bat swung it across the right side of Dad's head.

Dad stumbled back, sincerely dazed but still on his feet.

"Now stop it, Dad! I don't wanna fight you and I ain't stealin Don Knowles's pipe tonight!"

Dad, bleeding from his ears, turned and leveled Mike with another right hook.

"Like hell you're not, boy," he said as he prowled in on his son on the ground.

With the 2 x 4 out of distance and Dad bearing down on him again, Mike grabbed a hand full of sandy gravel from the ground and slung it across Dad's face, blinding him.

Dad stumbled back, struggling to get his bearings.

"That's enough, Pop! It's over!

But it wasn't. Unable to see, Dad lunged toward Mike's voice. Mike easily sidestepped him.

"That's enough, Dad!"

Dad, now a blind groveling bear with bleeding ears, came at Mike again.

"Where are you, boy? Where's my son who won't roll Don Knowles's pipe with his old man?"

Mike picked up the five-foot 2 x 4 and held it at the ready.

"Dad, I'm tellin ya, it's over. If you come at me again, I'm gonna knock you out with this 2 x 4." Dad heard him clearly, steadied himself, then said, "Give it your best shot, boy," as he blitzed Mike.

Whh-ooo-pp! The 2 x 4 went across Dad's head.

Out cold, Dad lay in a heap on the ground.

"Damnit, Dad?!" Mike said in shock, wondering if he'd killed him.

Mike, crying now, knelt down over Dad and yelled, "Damnit, Dad! I told you not to come at me again!"

Dad lay there, unmoving.

For four and a half minutes Mike knelt over his fallen pop, weeping.

"I didn't wanna do it, Dad, but you made me."

Dad then came to and slowly got to his feet.

"I'm sorry, Dad!" Mike shouted, "I'm sorry!"

My dad stood straight and wiped the gravel from his eyes. Mike, crying tears of shock and fear, readied himself for the risk of another round. Dad, eyes now clear, focused in on the young man who had just knocked him out cold, his first son.

The fight was over. Tears ran down my dad's face as well. But these were tears of pride and joy. Dad stepped toward Mike with open arms and took him into a loving bear hug, declaring into Mike's ear, "That's my boy, son, *that's* my boy."

From that day on Mike was an equal to Dad and Dad treated him as such. Dad never challenged Mike again, physically, morally, or philosophically. They were best of friends.

You see, rites of passage were a big deal to my dad, and if you were man enough to take him on, then you had to prove it. And Mike just did.

TO LOSE THE POWER OF CONFRONTATION IS TO LOSE THE POWER OF UNITY

Second in line to the privilege of my dad's methods of turning his boys into men was Pat. Over the past forty years, while Rooster has been chasing a career in the oil business in West Texas and I've been chasing one in Hollywood, Pat has been the fiercely loyal heartist of the family, the one who's always stayed closest to Mom. Growing up, he looked after me, took up for me, let me hang out with his friends, introduced me to rock 'n' roll, taught me how to golf, how to drive, how to ask a girl out on a date, and bought me my first beer.

Pat was *my* hero. His was Evel Knievel.

Pat's night with Dad came on a Friday in the early spring of 1969, eight months before I was magically born. Dad was out at Fred Smither's hunting camp with some friends a couple hours' drive from home. Their night's entertainment had segued into who could piss over whose head the highest. Each man, from shortest to tallest would stand on the barn wall, put a mark over his head, and the rest of them would see if they could flat-foot piss over the mark. Dad won when he was the only man who could piss six feet, four inches high, the mark he'd just put over his own head. The prize? Bragging rights.

But Dad wasn't the tallest man in the barn that night; at six foot, seven inches tall, Fred Smither was. And even though Dad had already won the contest, he had to see if he could piss over Fred's head. Fred stood up, marked the wall.

"C'mon, Big Jim! You can do it!" his buddies cheered. Pop chugged another beer, leaned back, and let it fly.

Nope, six four was as high as he could piss.

"I knew it, knew you couldn't piss over *my* head, Big Jim, hell, nobody can do *that*!" Fred Smither declared.

To which Dad quickly replied, "My boy can."

"Shit, Jim, ain't no way your boy or anyone else can piss over my head," Fred sneered.

"Like hell he can't; whadda you wanna bet?"

"Whadda *you* wanna bet?"

Dad eyed a used Honda XR-80 dirt bike leaning against a hay bale in the corner of the barn. You see, Pat had been asking for a dirt bike for Christmas all year long but Dad knew he couldn't afford to buy one, used or not.

"I'll bet you that little dirt bike over there my boy can piss over your head, Fred."

The gang all cracked up at the proposition. Fred looked at the dirt bike then back to Dad and said, "Deal, and if he don't, you owe me $200."

"I ain't got $200 to lose, Fred, but if my boy can't piss over your head, then you can keep my truck," Dad said.

"Deal," Fred replied.

"Deal. I'll be back with my boy by sunrise, don't y'all go to bed on me."

And with that, Dad hopped into his beat-up pickup truck and drove 112 miles back to our house in Uvalde to pick up Pat.

"Wake up, little buddy, wake up," Dad said as he quietly shook Pat from his slumber. "Put a coat and some shoes on, we're goin somewhere."

Eight-year-old Pat got out of bed, put on a pair of tennis shoes and a coat over his tighty-whities, then headed for the bathroom.

"No, no, no, son, I need you to hold it," Dad said as he rushed Pat out the door.

Dad drove Pat the 112 miles back to Fred Smither's hunting camp and made him drink two beers on the way. When they finally got to the camp at 4:40 in the morning, Pat's bladder was full of potential.

"Dad, I *really* gotta go bad."

"I know, I know, son, just hold it a few more minutes."

Dad and Pat, in his tennis shoes, coat, and tighty-whities, walked into the barn. The boys had quieted down but were still awake. Fred Smither, too.

"Boys, this is my son Pat, and he's about to piss over Fred's head!"

They all broke out in laughter again. Game on.

Fred sauntered over to the pissing wall, stood up tall, and chalked a fresh line above his head, all six foot seven of his height.

"What's goin on, Daddy?" Pat asked.

"You see that mark on the wall Mr. Fred just left?"

"Yes, sir."

"Think you can piss over it?"

"Hell yeah," Pat replied, then dropped his tighty-whities below his knees, put both hands on his pecker, aimed it at the mark, and let it fly.

Pat cleared Fred Smither's six-seven mark by two feet.

"That's my boy!! I told y'all my boy could piss over Fred's head!"

Dad hustled over to the corner of the barn, grabbed the Honda XR-80, and rolled it over to Pat.

"Merry Christmas, son!"

Then they loaded it in the back of Dad's truck, hopped in, and drove 112 miles back home just in time for breakfast.

Fourteen years later, Pat became the number one golfer on the Mississippi Delta State "Statesmen" golf team. A scratch golfer known as the "Texas Stallion," Pat had just won "low medalist" at the SEC tournament on the Arkansas Razorbacks' home course. The coach called a team meeting on the bus ride home. "Tomorrow morning, my house, eight A.M. sharp."

The next morning Coach gathered the team around him in his living room and said, "I have a concern that some players on our team were smoking marijuana in the city park of Little Rock yesterday before the tournament. Now, what we need to do is find out *who* it was that brought the marijuana from Delta State to Little Rock, *and who* was smoking it."

He was staring at Pat.

Pat, raised by my dad to know that telling the truth would save your ass, stepped forward.

"Coach, it was me. I brought the weed, and I smoked it."

Pat stood there, alone. None of the other teammates moved or said a word even though three of them had passed the doobie with him the other morning in Little Rock.

"Nobody else?" Coach asked.

Nothing.

"I'll let you know what my decision is tomorrow," Coach said. "You're dismissed."

The next morning, Coach showed up at Pat's dorm room.

"I'm telling your father *and* you're suspended from playing golf next semester."

Pat caught his breath. "Come on, Coach, I told you the truth . . . and I'm the best golfer on the team."

"Doesn't matter," Coach said. "You broke a team rule about drugs. You're suspended. And I'm going to tell your father."

"Look here, Coach," Pat said. "You can suspend me, but you **can't** tell my dad. You don't understand, a DWI you could call him about. But marijuana? He'll kill me." Pat had gotten busted with weed a couple times in his late teens, and after being on the receiving end of Dad's brand of discipline and disdain for *Mary Jane* before, he was going to make sure there wasn't a third.

"Well, that'll be between you and him." Coach didn't budge.

Pat inhaled deeply, "Okay, Coach, let's go for a ride."

They got in Pat's '81 Z28 and headed out for a drive across the Delta. After about ten minutes of silence Pat finally spoke up: "Let me make this real clear, Coach. You can suspend me, but if you call my dad . . . **I'll kill you.**"

Pat got suspended.

My dad never found out.

CONSERVATIVE early
Liberal late

Create structure so you can have freedom.

Create your weather so you can blow in the wind.

Map your direction so you can swerve in the lanes.

Clean up so you can get dirty.

Choreograph, then dance.

Learn to read and write before you start making up words.

Check if the pool has water in it before you dive in.

Learn to sail before you fly.

Initiation before inaugurations.

Earn your Saturdays.

We need discipline, guidelines, context, and responsibility early in any new endeavor. It's the time to sacrifice. To learn, to observe, to take heed.

If and when we get knowledge of the space, the craft, the people, and the plan, *then* we can let our freak flag fly, and create.

Creativity needs borders.

Individuality needs resistance.

The earth needs gravity.

Without them there is no form.

No art.

Only chaos.

As I said, I was an unplanned surprise—an *accident* as my mom still calls me—and my dad has always half jokingly told her, "That ain't my boy, Katy, that's *your* boy." Dad was on the road a lot when I was growing up, working to take care of the family, so I spent most of my time with Mom. It was true. I was a momma's boy. When I *did* get to spend time with Dad, I relished every moment.

I wanted and needed his approval, and on occasion he gave it to me. Other times, he'd rearrange my considerations in extremely colorful ways.

The best way to teach is the way that is most understood.

As a kid, my favorite TV show was *The Incredible Hulk* starring Lou Ferrigno.

I marveled at his muscles and would pose in front of the TV with my shirt off, arms bent, fists high, doing my best bulging body-builder biceps impersonation.

One night Dad saw me. "What are you doin, son?" he asked.

"One day I'm gonna have muscles like that, Dad," I said, motioning to the TV screen. "Big baseball-size biceps!"

Dad chuckled, then took off *his* shirt, matched my pose in front of the tube, and said, "Yeah, big biceps make the girls scream and they sure *look* good, but that ol' boy on the TV, he's so muscle-bound he can't even reach around to wipe his own ass . . . the biceps? They're just for *show*." He then slowly lowered both his arms in front of him, straightened them out with his fists to the floor, then he twisted his arms to the inside, and flexed a pair of massive triceps muscles.

"Now the *tri-ceps,* son," he said, this time pointing his nose back and forth toward the bulging muscles on the back of his upper arms, "*that's* the work muscle, that's the muscle that puts food on the table and the roof over your head. The tri-ceps? They're for *dough*." My dad would take the stockroom over the showroom any day.

It was the summer of 1979 when Dad moved Mom, me, and Pat from Uvalde, Texas (pop. 12,000), to the fastest-growing oil boom East Texas city in the nation, Longview (pop. 76,000). Where Uvalde taught me to deal, Longview taught me to dream.

Like everyone else, we moved for the money. Dad was still a pipe salesman, and Longview was the place to make it rich in the drilling business. Soon after arriving in town, Pat went away to a golf camp, and Mom went on an "extended vacation" at a beach house in Navarre Beach, Florida. Rooster, already a multimillionaire in his midtwenties, had moved to Midland, Texas, so it was just Dad and me living in a double-wide trailer on the outskirts of town.

My dad could hurt with his hands, but he could also heal with them. Painkillers were no match for his hands on my mom's head when she had migraines. Whether it was a broken arm or a broken heart, Dad's hands and his hugs could heal, especially when in service of an underdog or someone who couldn't help themselves.

The other inhabitant of that double-wide trailer Dad and I were living in that summer was a pet cockatiel named Lucky. Dad loved that bird and that bird loved Dad. He'd open her cage each morning and let her fly around the trailer, she'd roost on his shoulder while he walked around, and perch on his forearm while he petted her. He talked to Lucky. Lucky talked to him.

We only put Lucky back in her cage at night to sleep. The rest of the time, Lucky was loose in the trailer morning until night. The only rule was, you had to "*watch it*" when you exited or entered the door so Lucky didn't get out.

One late afternoon, after a July day of exploring the countryside on foot, I got back to the trailer at the same time Dad got home from work.

When we got inside, Lucky wasn't there to greet Dad like she always did. We looked all over. No Lucky. *Shit,* I thought, *did I accidentally let her out this morning when I left? Did anyone else come over today while we were gone?*

Seconds later, I heard Dad in the back of the trailer, "Oh god, oh god, noooo, Lucky."

I ran to the back and found Dad on his knees leaning over the toilet. There, floating in circles in the bottom of it, was Lucky. Tears dripping off his cheeks, Dad reached with both hands into the bottom of the bowl and gently cradled Lucky out. "Oh, no Lucky, noooo," he groaned through sobs. Lucky was dead. Soaking wet. Motionless. She must have accidentally fallen into the toilet and gotten stuck beneath the seat's edge trying to get out.

Dad, still weeping, brought Lucky's soggy and lifeless body closer to his face where he examined her hanging head. Then, he opened his mouth wide and slowly put Lucky into it until the bottom half of her wings and her tailfeathers were all that was outside it. He started to give Lucky mouth-to-mouth resuscitation. Only breathing through his nose so to keep constant airflow into her lungs, he made sure his breath was measured, enough, he hoped, to revive her, but not so much to burst her tiny lungs. On his knees, over a toilet, cradling the bottom half of a cockatiel named Lucky with the top half of the same bird in his mouth, he breathed into her with the perfect amount of pressure. One exhale . . . Two exhales . . . Three exhales. His tears soaking the already saturated bird. Four exhales . . . Five . . . A feather quivered . . . Six exhales . . . Seven . . . A wingtip fluttered. Eight . . . Dad lightly loosened his grip and released some pressure from his lips. Nine . . .

Another wing tried to flap. He opened his mouth slightly wider. Ten . . . And that's when we heard, coming from inside my father's mouth, *a small chirp*. Now, with tears of pain turning to tears of joy, Dad gently removed Lucky's torso and head from his mouth. Lucky twitched some toilet water and saliva off her head. Now face-to-face, they looked into each other's eyes. She *was* dead. Now she was alive. Lucky lived another eight years.

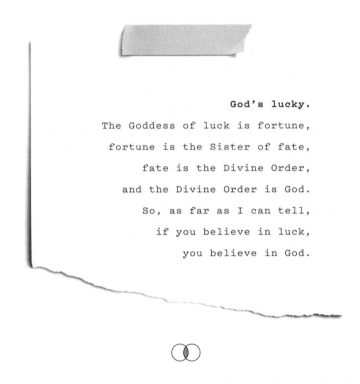

God's lucky.
The Goddess of luck is fortune,
fortune is the Sister of fate,
fate is the Divine Order,
and the Divine Order is God.
So, as far as I can tell,
if you believe in luck,
you believe in God.

That same summer, while Dad was at work every day, I explored the endless acres of the Piney Woods, barefoot and shirtless, wearing a shammy roped around my waist, with my Daisy BB gun in hand. Coming from Uvalde, I'd never seen trees like this. Towering pines shooting straight up into the sky, thousands of them. I was in awe of one in particular, a white pine among the ponderosa, six feet wide at its base, its peak trespassing the airspace.

One late afternoon while chasing down a squirrel with my Daisy a half mile from home, I came across a fence, about ten feet tall. It was strangled with vines and overgrowth and a few faded No Trespassing signs. I crouched, pulled back some foliage, and peeked through. On the other side was a lumberyard. Men in hard hats, a couple of forklifts in action, and mountainous stacks of 2 x 4's, 4 x 4's, and plywood. *Perfect,* I thought. *For a tree house.*

And I knew just the tree. I stayed there until they shut down the forklifts, packed up, and closed down for the day. It was about 6:00 P.M. I ran home with a plan. A plan I couldn't tell Dad. A plan for the next three months of my summer.

The next morning after breakfast, Dad went to work at 6:30 like he always did. As soon as he left, I went to our toolbox and found what I was looking for, a pair of wire cutters. I put on my shammy, grabbed my Daisy, left my shoes in the closet, and ran to scope out my mark.

How was I gonna do this? There were people working at the lumberyard all day, so I'd have to come at night, I plotted. What if I got caught by someone at the lumberyard? What if I got caught sneaking out at night by Dad? And what if he then found out I was stealing lumber from a lumberyard half a mile from home? I was nervous. I was excited.

That night after dinner and watching *The Incredible Hulk* like I always did, Dad and I said our good nights. I lay in bed, wondering how long I should wait before I opened the double-wide bedroom window to sneak out. I could hear Dad still moving around on his end of the trailer so I waited until the slightest creaks had been silent for at least an hour before I made my move. Slowly, quietly, I got out of bed. I wrapped on my shammy skirt, left my shoes in the closet, grabbed my Daisy, a small flashlight, and the wire cutters. I tossed them all carefully out the window onto the lawn below, then snuck myself out the window and headed to my secret stash.

It was around 1:00 A.M. I figured I should be back home in bed before five, so I had a few hours to work. The yard was quiet. I threw a couple of rocks over the fence to see if any guard dogs were around. Nothing. I pulled back some vines and bushes, then, with the flashlight between my chin and chest, I brought the wire cutters to the first chain link with both hands. *Clip.* It took all my double-fisted might to cut through it. *Clip. Clip. Clip. Clip.* Until I had cleared a space about six feet wide and a foot tall—wide enough to get those plywood planks through, small enough to go unnoticed. I hoped.

Adrenaline pumping, I lay on my back and shimmied under the fence onto the private property. I went to the stack of 4 x 4's, pulled one off, and dragged it to the opening in the fence. I pushed it through as far as I could, then crawled under the fence and pulled it out from the other side, where I then dragged it the few hundred yards deep into the forest and left it at the base of *the big white pine.* Then I ran back to steal the next one. Once I got my second load to the tree, it was already a little after 4:30 A.M. so I raced back to the fence, replaced all the brush and vines to conceal the hole I'd cut, then ran back home. I snuck in the window, put my Daisy and the flashlight back on the shelf and the wire cutters under my mattress, got under the covers, and slept until Dad woke me up at 6:00 to make breakfast.

It went on like that for over a month. Getting little sleep at night, I'd take catnaps under that white pine next to my growing stack of lumber during the day, then make it home for dinner, and do it all over again. I did this every night until I had enough 2 x 4's, 4 x 4's, and plywood planks to build the biggest and tallest tree house in the world.

With the most dangerous part of my plan behind me and two months of summer left, it was time to start construction. I'd also stolen about forty feet of 15-gauge Steel Trim Pin Nail gun nails from the yard and I already had a hammer and a twenty-six-inch handsaw from our toolbox at home. All I needed was daylight.

Up at six and out the door by seven, I worked on that tree house until dark seven days a week for the next two months. Shirtless and shoeless in my shammy I crisscrossed two paper collated clips of the nails over my shoulders and across my chest. Half Comanche Indian, half Pancho Villa, with hammer in hand, I went to work. I started with the bottom floor then built up. I cut a two-by-two-foot hole in each floor next to the trunk of the tree where I nailed pieces of 2 x 4's for ladder steps to get from floor to floor. I also made a pulley system that I raised with each floor. I'd pack my lunch each morning and take it to *my* construction site, put my brown bag in the trough, climb up to the highest floor, and hoist my sandwich up to eat during my lunch break.

Six weeks later when I was done, my tree house was thirteen stories high.

The thirteenth floor was over one hundred feet above the ground. From there I could see all the way to downtown Longview, fifteen miles away. For the next two weeks I spent every day up there, above the rest of the world, where I hoisted up my brown bag lunch and daydreamed, swearing I could see the earth's curve on the horizon, now understanding where and why the city of Longview got its name.

It was the best summer of my life.

GREENLIGHT.

Then September came and I had to go back to school. Mom came back from Florida and we soon moved into a neighborhood house on the other side of town. I never saw that tree house again.

I often wonder if it's still there today. I thought of that tree house when I was making the movie *Mud*. My tree house was those boys' "Boat in a Tree." A secret, a mystery, a place of danger, wonder, and dreams. If *Mud* had been released in 1979, my dad would have come to me and said, "Hey, buddy, there's this movie called *Mud* I saw, we gotta watch it together, damn it's a good one." Then I might have said to him, "Dad, there's this tree house in the woods I built, I gotta show it to you, damn it's a good one."

Oh yeah, that "extended vacation" in Florida my mom was on? It would be twenty years before I learned that in fact she was not on vacation, rather, she and Dad were in the middle of their second divorce.

IT'S NOT VANITY, IT'S COMMERCE. (UNTIL IT'S VANITY AGAIN?)

During high school, we still lived in that same house on the other side of town in Longview. Mom had just started selling a product called "Oil of Mink," a facial cosmetic that she peddled door to door. It was touted as a *breakthrough skin care treatment* that would "bring out all the impurities in your skin" and "saturate your face with beautiful mink oil so you would have a clear, glowing complexion for the rest of your life."

At the same time, I was entering adolescence—you know, pubic hairs growing in, balls dropping, voice lowering, and . . . a few pimples.

One day my mom looked at my face and said, "You should use the Oil of Mink!"

A fan of self-regard and looking my best, I listened to her and started applying Oil of Mink to my face each night before bed. The result? *More* pimples.

"It must be bringing out the impurities!" Mom said.

I listened to her again and continued to slather more Oil of Mink on my face each night.

A week went by. *More* pimples.

Twelve days passed. Now I had what looked like full-blown acne.

"Mom, are you sure this is okay for me to be using?" I asked.

"Of course it is, but let's call my boss, Elaine, to come over and have a look just to be sure."

Elaine came over and took a look at my swollen, zit-infested face.

"Oh, wow!" she shrieked. "Yes, the product is doing *exactly* what it's supposed to do. It's bringing out all the impurities! And my oh my, you must just have a lot of impurities, Matthew! Just keep applying the Oil of Mink each night, and eventually it'll pull *all* the impurities out, and then you'll have a clear, glowing complexion for the rest of your life."

Well, shit, okay. Sounded like I just needed to weather the storm. I stayed at it.

Three weeks in, my entire cheeks were swollen, red pustules. Huge whiteheads. Blistering geysers of pus. I looked like a different person.

Against my mother's counsel, I decided to see a dermatologist. Dr. Haskins looked at my face. "Oh my, Matthew, what the . . . the pores on your face are clogged and holding oil and grease in. There's no room for them to breathe. What are you putting on your face?" he asked.

I pulled out a bottle of the Oil of Mink. He examined the label.

"How long you been using this product, Matthew?"

"Twenty-one days."

"Oh my god, no, no, no! This is for people that are at least over forty years old, definitely *not* for a teenager going through adolescence when your skin is secreting more oil. This product has completely blocked your pores, Matthew; you have severe nodular acne. You are ten days away from having ice-pick scars in your cheeks for the rest of your life. I am going to prescribe you a pill called Accutane. Hopefully we've caught it in enough time that the Accutane will dry you out to such an extent that maybe you can get rid of the acne within a year and hopefully not have lifelong damage."

"Well, that Oil of Mink didn't work at *all,* did it, Matthew?!" Mom innocently proclaimed.

"No, Mom . . . it didn't."

I immediately got *off* the Oil of Mink and got *on* the Accutane, which came with its own set of side effects. After a few weeks, my skin started drying out, my face began to scale and flake, the creases in my lips dried up and bled, my knees got arthritic, I got headaches, my hair started falling out, I got hypersensitive allergic reactions, and I looked like a swollen prune. All side effects I was more than happy to live with to get rid of my Oil of Mink–induced acne.

But that's not the end of the story. No, not in the McConaughey household. My dad smelled an opportunity.

"We're gonna sue em!!! That goddamn Oil of Mink company! That's what we'll do. We're gonna sue em and make some money off this whole deal. I mean, look at you, son, that product should have never been given out to you, boy, and that lady Elaine, she shouldn't have been telling your mother to give it to you! I'm tellin ya, we got a case."

Dad took me to meet his lawyer, Jerry Harris, a good-looking, erudite middle-aged man who had an air of confidence about him that made you think he was from Dallas, not Longview.

"Damn right, we got a case," Jerry said. "This product should have never been administered to a teenager, there's no disclaimer or warning on the bottle about its possible harms either, and I am sure that besides all of the physical pain you're goin through . . ."

Jerry and my dad homed in on me.

"You *are* under great *emotional distress* as well, aren't you, Matthew?"

"Uhh . . . yes."

Jerry pulled out a cassette recorder and pressed the red button.

"Yes, what?" he asked.

"I am . . . under great emotional distress at this time."

"Why?" he asked, nodding.

"Because . . . I now have bad acne on my face that I never had before using this Oil of Mink product?"

"Exactly," Jerry said, "and has this predicament affected your confidence?"

"Yes, sir."

"In what way?"

"It's lower."

"Good. Has it affected your relationship with the girls?"

"I mean, I was doing really good with the girls *before* I had the acne, and I'm not doing as well now."

"Exactly," Jerry said, stopping the tape recorder.

"We got a case, Jim. Emotional distress is a strong tack for prosecution, and hell, look at him, he's all swole up, looks like shit. I think we can get thirty-five to fifty grand out of this deal."

A big gunslinger's grin spread across Dad's face. He gave Jerry a heavy attaboy handshake and patted me on the back.

"Good job, boy, good job."

Well, as you know, lawsuits take a while. Two years had passed since the Oil of Mink applications, and with my acne long gone, not a pimple on my face, and no side effects in sight, the Accutane had worked. I was now being called into a deposition with the defense attorney representing Oil of Mink. Cassette recorder on the desk, red button pressed.

"Matthew, how are you, son?"

"I'm doin better, thank you."

"I'm just so sorry that this all happened to you, Matthew, it must have been such an emotionally distressful time for you."

I couldn't believe it. The defense attorney just lobbed me a softball and I was ready to crush it over the fence.

"Oh, yes, sir. It *was* an emotionally distressful time. I mean, I looked like the Elephant Man, and my scalp was dry, my hair was falling out, my knees hurt, my back hurt, my face flaked, I didn't have any confidence, and I wasn't doing any good with the girls. I mean, that Oil of Mink almost scarred me for life."

"Oh, bless your heart, young man. I can only imagine how tough it must've been and *still is* on you."

I doubled down, "Yes, sir, that's right."

He stared at me a moment and then the slightest Cheshire grin began to creep up on his lips as he reached under the table and pulled out a high school yearbook—*my* high school yearbook—from that year,

1988. He slowly opened it and turned to a flagged page, swiveled the book around to face me and slid it in my direction. Then, reaching across the table, he put his finger on a particular picture and said, "Is this you?"

It was. It was a picture of me with Camissa Springs. We both had a silk sash draped across our chests from shoulder to hip. Hers read "Most Beautiful." Mine read "Most Handsome."

Shit. I knew right then and there our case was done. He had me.

"Scarred for life, huh? . . . Sooooo emotionally distressed," he said, as his grin got wider.

I was right. We were done. Case dropped.

My dad was inconsolable, he went on about it for weeks, muttering "Goddamn you, boy!!! Here I am, I got a chance to make thirty-five to fifty thousand dollars on a lawsuit that we *coulda* won!!! And you gotta go off and win 'Most Handsome'! You screwed up the whole lawsuit, son! Damn you, boy!"

Most Beautiful is Camissa Springs and Most Handsome is Matthew McConaughey.

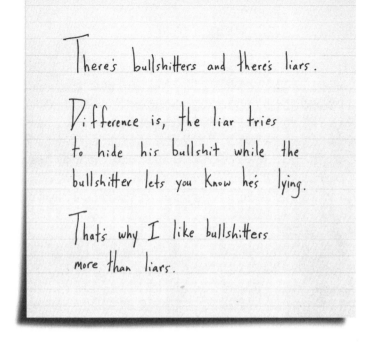

There's bullshitters and there's liars.

Difference is, the liar tries
to hide his bullshit while the
bullshitter lets you know he's lying.

That's why I like bullshitters
more than liars.

A few months later, with Mom on her second *extended vacation* to Navarre Beach (not another divorce, just a little "break" from each other), it was just Dad and me living together again, this time in our three-bedroom house instead of the double-wide. I got home by my midnight curfew. Unexpectedly, Dad was awake, and on the phone.

"Sure, Mr. Felker, he just got in. Lemme ask him," I heard him say as I entered his bedroom. The lights were on and he was sitting on the side of his bed in his underwear. He lowered the phone from his ear and held it between his neck and shoulders.

"What'd you do tonight, son?"

I should have known I was busted but instead chose to try and hustle the man who had taught me to hustle.

"Uh, not much, me and Bud Felker went to Pizza Hut then he dropped me off here at home," I said.

"You pay for that pizza, son?"

He was giving me a second chance to come clean and avoid getting punished for the one thing worse than getting *caught* misbehaving, lying about it. But rather than admitting what I had done, and instinctually knew *he* knew I had done, I chose to double down on my grovel.

"Well, I think so, Dad . . . I mean, I went to the car before Bud, and I'm pretty sure he was supposed to pay for it."

Digging my own grave, I was in too deep to climb out now.

Dad took a deep breath, a delayed blink, and looked distraught for a moment, then he lifted the phone back to his ear.

"Mr. Felker, thank you, sir, I'll handle mine from here," then he placed the phone back in its holster.

I was now starting to sweat.

Dad calmly put his hands on his knees and raised his chin to look me in the eye when I saw his molars meet.

"I'm gonna ask you one more time like this, son: Did you *know* you were gonna steal that pizza?"

All I had to do was say, "Yes, sir, Dad, I did," and he would have only cussed me about not committing a crime thoroughly enough to get away with it and lashed my ass with his leather belt a couple of times because I got caught, but no.

My eyes widened, a quarter-sized spot of urine now showing on the crotch of my jeans, I stuttered, "No, sir, li-like I said I . . ."

Whoppp!! The back of my father's right hand crashed across my face as he leapt from the bed and interrupted my pitiful plea. I hit the ground, not so much from the force of his strike as from the instability of the cowardly, panic-stricken, lactic acid legs I was wobbling on.

I deserved it. I earned it. I asked for it. I wanted it. I needed it. I got it.

I lied to him, and it broke his heart.

Stealing a pizza was no big deal to him, he'd stolen plenty of pizzas in his life and then some. All I had to do was admit it. But I didn't.

56

Now on my knees crying from shock and fear just like my brother Mike had done but for different reasons, I was ashamed. Unlike him at the barn, I was a rat, a fink, a *pussy,* a coward.

That's not my boy, Katy, that's yours, is all I could hear in my mind.

He stood over me.

"The waitress at the Pizza Hut recognized Bud. She looked up his number and called his house, asked his dad to have him just bring the money for the pizza by tomorrow. Bud told his dad it was all his idea to steal it and that you just went along with it. But you *lied* to me, son, told me you didn't know."

All he wanted me to do was stand up like a man, admit I had fucked up, look him in the eye, and shake it off, but no.

I cowered, made excuses, and whimpered as he looked down on me. The piss stain on my jeans now spread to my leg.

Getting more furious with my spinelessness, he dropped on all fours like a bear in front of me, then taunted me, "C'mon, I'll give you four to my one. Four of your best shots across my kisser to one of mine across yours!"

Paralyzed, numb, I didn't take the offer. The idea of striking my dad made my hands feel like papier-mâché. The thought of him striking me again made my brain drain.

"Why?! Why?!" he raged.

Unable to answer, I just stumbled to knee level and crawled to the nearest corner where I stayed until he finally stood up and shook his head at me, wondering what he'd done wrong to raise such a coward of a son.

I've often regretted what I did—or didn't do—that night.

I had my chance at my rite of passage—to become *his boy* or a *man* in his eyes—but I got stage fright, pissed my pants, and failed the test. I choked.

FIND YOUR
FREQUENCY

MY SENIOR YEAR IN HIGH school. I was rolling. I had straight A's, a job that kept forty-five bucks in my back pocket at all times, a four handicap in golf, I'd won "Most Handsome" in my class, and was dating the best-looking girl at my school *and* at the school across town. Yeah, I was catching greenlights.

Never the too-cool-for-school guy who leans against the wall and smokes a cigarette at the party, no, I was the guy who danced at the party. The guy who *chased* the girls and worked his way to the front row of every concert, no matter how late I arrived. I gave effort. I was a hustler.

I drove a truck. I took the girls *off-road muddin** after school in that truck. I had a megaphone in the front grille, and in the school parking lot in the mornings, I'd crouch down in the cab and say through the speaker, *"Look at the jeans Cathy Cook's got on today, lookin goooooood!"*

Everyone loved it. Everyone laughed. Especially Cathy Cook.

I was *that* guy. I was the fun guy. I engaged.

---

* Four-wheel driving through the soggy-bottom creeks of East Texas.

61

One day I was driving past our local Nissan dealership and I saw a candy-red 300ZX for sale.

I'd never had a sports car before, and this one even had T-tops.

I pulled my truck onto the lot to inquire. The dealer was motivated to sell.

On the spot, I traded my truck in for that candy-red 300ZX . . . with T-tops.

I had a red sports car.

Every Sunday afternoon I'd polish and wax that red sports car. It was my baby.

At school, I started parking in the *third* parking lot, that empty lot way in the back, where no other car doors could dent or scratch my new baby's paint.

I knew the chicks were going to dig my red sports car even more than my truck, and hence, dig me more. I'd arrive early to school every morning, park in that *third* parking lot, and just *leeeaaan* against it.

I was *so* cool.

My red sports car was *so* cool.

A few weeks passed and I started noticing some changes. The chicks, they weren't digging me like they used to. It was like they were bored with me *leeeaaanin* against my red sports car.

After school they went *muddin off road* in someone else's truck instead of *cruisin the streets T-tops down* with me.

I wasn't getting near as many dates as I used to. The girls seemed to lose interest in me.

What happened? I wondered.

Then one day it hit me.

I lost my truck.

I lost the effort, the hustle, the mudding, and the megaphone. I lost *the fun*.

I was too busy *leeeaaanin* against that candy-red 300ZX with T-tops in the third parking lot.

I'd gotten lazy, started looking in the mirror at my hair too often, relying on that red sports car to do the work *for* me, and it was doing a shitty job.

I'd outfoxed myself when I'd traded in my truck for that red sports car, and I lost my mojo when I did.

The next day after school, I went back to that Nissan dealership and traded it back in for my truck.

The day after that I pulled into the first parking lot again, flirted with the ladies from the megaphone, and took them *off-road muddin* after school.

And like clockwork, I was *back*.

Fuckin red sports car.

GREENLIGHT.

process of elimination and identity

The first step that leads to our identity in life is usually not *I know who I am,* but rather *I know who I'm not.* Process of elimination.

Too many options can make a tyrant out of any of us, so we should get rid of the excess in our lives that keep us from being more of ourselves. When we decrease the options that don't feed us, we eventually, almost accidentally, have more options in front of us that *do.*

Knowing who we are is hard. Eliminate who we're *not* first, and we'll find ourselves where we need to be.

On my eighteenth birthday, my parents said to me, "If you haven't learned it yet, you're not going to." In my family, the eighteenth birthday was a seminal moment. It meant no more rules. It meant no more curfew. It meant independence. It meant freedom.

I graduated from high school, and like most kids, I wasn't sure what I wanted to do with the rest of my life. I mean, I *thought* I wanted to go to law school and become a defense attorney, but I wasn't absolutely certain. My mom came up with this radical idea: "Hey, you love to travel, Matthew. What if you become an exchange student?"

Immediately I was up for it. "Sounds adventurous and wild, I'm in."

We went to the local Rotary Club that ran the exchange program and learned that they had two openings for a foreign exchange: one to Sweden and one to Australia. Sun, beaches, surfing, Elle Macpherson, English-speaking—I chose Australia.

Next thing I knew I was sitting at a boardroom table in front of twelve suits at the local Rotary Club. After they approved my background papers, a man said, "We think you'd be a great ambassador of the State of Texas and the United States in the faraway land of Australia. We'd love for you to go, but before you do, we need you to sign this paper saying you will not come back until your full year of this exchange is over."

That seemed odd. "But I *am* going the whole year, that's the plan."

"Everyone says that," he retorted. "But the reason we need you to sign this contract is because every exchange student gets severely homesick and tries to come home early. We can't have that happen, which is why we need you to sign this document stating that, 'I, Matthew McConaughey, promise not to come home early unless there is a tragedy or death in my family.'"

"Look," I said, "I'm *not* signing that paper, but I'll shake on it. I'm not gonna quit and come home, I'm in for the entire year." I looked him in the eye. "Deal?"

He agreed, we shook, and soon I was packing up to go to Australia for a full year. I'd leave in ten days.

A few days later I got my first letter from my Australian host family, the Dooleys. It read:

"We can't wait to meet you and are so looking forward to having you in our home, Matthew. We live in paradise. Near the beach, on the outskirts of Sydney, you're going to love it."

Yes. Outstanding. Everything I was hoping for—the beach, Sydney—this was going be a blast. *Australia, here I come.*

Matthew McConaughey

District 583
1988–89   Australia

2023 Oak Forest Place
Longview, Texas 75605
U.S.A.
Telephone: 214-297-4462

Day 1

I arrived at the Sydney International Airport terminal. Duffel bag over my shoulder, I was walking down a long ramp toward a huge room with thousands of people awaiting their arrivals when I heard, through the sea of people chatting and greeting their guests, "Matthew! Matthew! Matthew!" My eyes went to the sound. I saw a hand popping up and down above all the other heads and moving toward the end of the ramp, "Matthew! Matthew! Matthew!"

As I reached floor level, the owner of that bouncing hand who was yelling my name was there to greet me. With an eager smile he lowered that hand and I shook it. Meet Norvel Dooley. Five foot four, 220 pounds, mustache, balding head, and a bit of an English accent I would later come to find out was an affectation he used to appear more *proper*. "Awww, there he is, look at him, strong, handsome American boy. Welcome to Australia, son! You're gonna love it."

He introduced me to his wife, Marjorie. Wearing a white polyester dress with big green polka dots, she was four foot ten, and using a walker because of a kyphotic spinal deformity (which back then we'd have called a hunchback). I leaned down and gave her a big hug and kiss, and she reached up and held my face in her hands, then warmly said, "Welcome to Australia, Matthew. Welcome to your new family; meet my son Michael." His shirt buttoned down and tucked in with a pocket protector, Michael wore a key ring around his right belt loop that held fifty keys, forty-eight of which I would later find out were unnecessary, but like his father's accent, healthy for his ego. As I reached out to shake his hand, he sidestepped it in favor of a hearty embrace, before he stepped back and began giving me extremely firm stiff-arm slaps to the middle of my back, singing, "My little brother! My little brother!"

Meet the Dooleys.

We loaded into the car and left the airport. I was riding shotgun, Norvel was driving, Marjorie and Michael were in the back seat. After about an hour, I noticed the skyline of the metropolitan city of Sydney was well behind us in the rearview mirror. Even the *outskirts* seemed out of sight. I asked Norvel, "So . . . technically, it's not Sydney that you live in, right?"

"No, mate," he proudly replied. "That's the big city. Sin, sin, sin going on over there, mate. You don't want to be living there, it's no place for civilized men. We actually live in a little place down the road here called Gosford on the Central Coast. Great spot, beautiful beaches, you're gonna love it."

We continued our small talk and drove another forty minutes when we made it to Gosford. Its population looked to be a couple hundred thousand; it was on the coast with miles of beaches, a pretty happening place. "*This* is going to work, beautiful," I said aloud. They said nothing.

We continued driving through downtown another fifteen to twenty minutes when I noticed Gosford was now in the rearview mirror. Odd. I once again respectfully asked, "So . . . it's not actually Gosford that you live in, is it?" To which Norvel once again protested with pride, "Oh, no, still a bit too citified, mate, loose morals; country livin's a lot better than that place. We actually live just down the road here a bit in a place called Toukley. You're gonna love it."

We drove another forty minutes then got to the town of Toukley. Population 5,000. It had one red light, one bar, and one small supermarket, but it was still on the coast, and a very pretty place. "Okay," I said aloud, "small-town livin, reminds me of where I was born, I can dig it." They had no comment. Norvel continued driving.

We drove six or seven more minutes and came to the roundabout on the other side of town. Now quite confused, I asked, "So . . . it's not really Toukley that you live in either?" Without hesitation and with just as much determination Norvel replied, "Nah, Toukley's a nice spot, mate, but a bit big for our taste. We actually live in a little gaff down the road here a bit, Matthew, beautiful little spot called Gorokan. You're gonna love it."

The pavement turned to blacktop.

A few minutes later we then came upon Gorokan, population 1,800, a sleepy inland one-street country town. No beach in sight. A couple of small one-story wooden houses to the right and left of Main Street. I took a semideep breath and before I knew it we were going through another roundabout on the other side of town, the blacktop turned to dirt road, and Gorokan was in the rearview mirror.

Now a bit peeved, I stated more than I asked, "So . . . you don't live in Gorokan, either, do you?"

"No." Norvel grunted with excitement. "But we're veee-rry close, mate, just down the trail here a spell, beautiful little country spot, mate, you're gonna love it."

We drove down that dusty trail for about five miles. I was staring out the window at the countryside, trying to recalibrate my expectations, when a green roadside sign intercepted my view. It read WAR-NERVALE, POP. 305. With no civilization in view, we drove another mile past that sign, and took the first left turn we could, then the first right, then pulled into a gravel driveway up to the garage door of the only house in sight, came to a stop, and turned off the ignition, when Norvel said with great fanfare, "Welcome to Australia, Matthew. You're gonna love it."

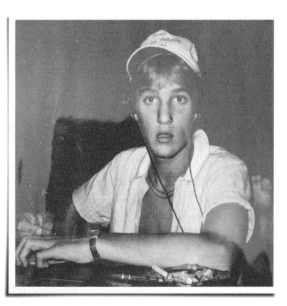

Day 4

I was washing after-dinner dishes when Norvel and Marjorie entered the kitchen. "Matthew, we'd like to have our extended family over this weekend and we thought you could cook us something, maybe something quintessentially American."

"I'd love to," I said. *But what to cook,* I wondered. "Ah, nothing more American than a hamburger, that's it, we're having good old American hamburgers this weekend."

"Top choice, Matthew," Norvel said as they turned to leave.

"Actually, no!" I raised my voice. "I take that back. We're having cheeseburgers, cus *the man who invented the hamburger was smart, but the man who invented the cheeseburger was a genius.*"

I started writing down a grocery list for my culinary masterpiece— soft white buns, dill pickle slices, cheddar and American cheese, red onion, avocado, jalapeños, real mayonnaise, good ketchup—when I felt a tap on my shoulder. It was Norvel.

"Matthew, would you come with me, please? I'd like to talk to you for a second." We exited the kitchen, walked across the living room, and down a hallway where he opened the second door on the right. "This way, please," he said as he ushered me into the room. It was his office. He then shut the door behind us and pointed to the seat in front of the desk. I sat down. He then went behind the desk and stepped up onto a platform where his chair was perched, then sat in it.

Oddly, Norvel, who was five foot four, was now sitting about a foot and a half higher than I was. He settled in and leaned forward. Placing his elbows on the desk, he crossed his hands knuckle for knuckle, looked me in the eye, and sternly said, "Matthew, I'd like to talk to you about your choice of words."

"Yes, sir," I said, "whadda you got?"

Chin on those knuckles, he turned his eyes to a portrait of Winston Churchill on the wall, took a composing inhale, and said, "YOU said that the man who invented the hamburger was smart, but the man who invented the cheeseburger was a genius, did you not?"

"Yes, sir, I did say that."

He took another aristocratic breath. "Matthew . . . that is merely your opinion. And in your time here with us, you will learn to appreciate fine wines, fine cheeses, and NOT to voice your opinion for the masses."

"Norvel, it's a figure of speech," I said. "It just basically means I like cheeseburgers more than hamburgers."

"Ah!, ah!, ah!" he chided as he waved his finger at me. "As I said, for the duu-ration of your stay in Australia, with us here in the Dooley household, you will learn to appreciate fine wines, fine cheeses, and NOT to voice your opinion for the masses."

He was dead serious.

Other than the Dooleys thinking that more than a couple of hours away was still the *outskirts of Sydney,* this nonsensical lecture was the first odd thing that happened to me in Australia.

I was puzzled, but I chalked it up to "cultural differences."

Day 8

I started school.

I had already graduated in America, but this school decided to enroll me with the junior class since I had arrived midterm. The thinking was, I could go into my senior term next year with the same group of kids.

Two weeks into the curriculum the year-and-a-half-old syllabus seemed like a breeze to me. Math was so easy it was boring, but I was enjoying my creative writing in the English classes. The teachers, on the other hand, were not. They red-pen marked up everything I wrote and gave me F minuses across the board because of my use of contractions, euphemisms, made-up words, and occasional profanity.

"Look, I know *how* to write, I passed those tests. I am deliberately writing how I am, I'm being creative, expressing myself," I said. Their response? "F minus!"

Socially the school was awkward as well. Everyone wore uniforms and played tag at lunch. No one had a driver's license, no one wanted to party, and the chicks were not digging me. I felt like I was back in junior high. I started missing my truck, my friends, those girlfriends, my freedom, Texas. But I told myself everything was fine, all part of the adventure—*cultural differences.*

I soon started skipping class daily and going to the library instead, where I discovered the great English poet Lord Byron. I had three cassettes: INXS's *Kick,* Maxi Priest's *Maxi/Maxi Priest,* and U2's *Rattle and Hum.* [*] I'd listen to them on my Walkman while I read about romance.

Two weeks later the principal came to me in the library. "Matthew," he said, "it doesn't seem like this school thing is working out for you, mate. I was thinking that maybe you could transfer into our *work experience* program where you would practice a trade off campus. You wouldn't get paid, but you *would* get school credit."

Fuck yes. "I'm in," I said.

My first job was as a bank teller at the Australia and New Zealand Bank. Being around adults was refreshing. I became friends with the manager of the bank, Connor Harrington; we enjoyed lunches and a few pints together after work.

Back home with the Dooleys, peculiar things were still happening.

Per usual, we ate an early dinner, 5:00–5:30 P.M. at the Dooley household. It was always me, Norvel, Marjorie, Michael, and Michael's girlfriend, Meredith, at the dinner table in the kitchen. Meredith was twenty-two years old and had a slight developmental disability that didn't allow her to drive a motor vehicle. She also had a habit of five-finger squeezing the whitehead pimples that were sometimes on her cheeks when she got nervous. I liked Meredith, we got along well, and she had a great sense of humor.

---

[*] Still one of my all-time favorites.

71

While at the dinner table one late afternoon, I had the Summer Olympics on the television just in view from the living room. The US was about to race in the finals of the Women's 4 x 100 meter relay. I seemed to be the only one interested. *Bang!* The starting gun went off and less than forty-two seconds later the US women had won gold. I clenched my fist in pride and patriotism and let out a muttered "Yes!," mostly to myself.

Norvel evidently saw this as an ideal moment for a history lesson. He leapt from his chair and scampered into the living room where he shut *off* the TV mid-post-race celebration and then marched back to the kitchen. Standing over me, he said, "Matthew, would you come with me, please, I'd like to talk to you for a second." Uh-oh. He escorted me out of the kitchen, across the living room, and down the hallway to the second door on the right. Yes, *back* to his office where this time he grabbed an encyclopedia off his bookshelf, sat upon his high chair, glanced at Winston on the wall, opened the encyclopedia to a dog-eared page, and began to lecture me. "A *real* athlete, Matthew, a *great* athlete, was this young chap from Great Britain named David Broome, who, in the 1960 Summer Olympics, won a bronze medal in the equestrian event of show jumping!"

"Okay, that's cool, Norvel," I said.

"And another thing, Matthew, that silly movie *Stripes* you were watching the other night—it's brainless and imma-*tur*! It is a *fuu*-rther example of the inferiority of American humor to that of the English."

Wow. "Okay . . . Mind if I go finish watching the Olympics?"

I was starting to feel pretty uncomfortable at the Dooleys. *But hey,* I told myself again, *it's just cultural differences*.

Day 90

Now getting my work experience as a barrister's assistant, I was enjoying my days in court, helping write closing arguments, studying the jury, researching law history, and taking notes for the jurist I was assisting. It was also great preparation for my future plans to become a lawyer. Still, back at the Dooleys, the *cultural differences* were starting to get to me.

My identity shaken, I needed some resistance to find my footing, something to overcome, a discipline to adhere to, a sense of purpose, so I could better maintain my sanity in the strange place I was in. I decided to become a vegetarian. The problem was, I didn't know how to be a vegetarian, so I began eating a head of iceberg lettuce with ketchup on it for dinner every night.

I also began running six miles a day after work. I got very thin.

I also decided to become abstinent for the rest of the year, which still had nine months in it.

I started to believe that my life's calling was to become a monk.

I made plans to go to South Africa after my year's exchange and free Nelson Mandela.

I wrote letters to my mom and dad, friends, and old girlfriends. My very first letter, which I wrote my first week at the Dooleys', was scrawled in a big black Sharpie,

"Hey, throwin some shrimp on the barbie. Love you, Matthew."

But now, my letters were becoming nine, ten, eleven, twelve, sixteen pages long, with minute and meticulous handwriting and eight-line run-on sentences full of too many adjectives and adverbs. Other than my mom, my childhood friend Robb Bindler was the only one who would write me back. A writer himself, he accepted my manic filibusters on the page and returned them with equal length but less derangement. Mostly though, I wrote to myself.

But I was fine, right? Just a little homesickness. *Cultural differences.* I got this. . . .

boundaries to freedom

We need finites, borders, gravity,
demarcations, shape, and resistance, to have
order.

This order creates responsibility.

The responsibility creates judgment.

The judgment creates choice.

In the **choice** lies the freedom.

To create the weather that gives us the most
favorable wind

we must first remove that which causes the
most friction to our core being.

This process of elimination **creates order**
by default, therefore rendering **more** to go
toward, for instance, and **less** to back away
from.

We then embrace these affirmations because
doing so brings us pleasure and less pain.

So we cultivate them until they become
habits, and form our **constitution**,

then they **proliferate** and become **emanations
of our essence**.

This is where true **identity** is born.

We fool ourselves in freedom if we think it
means getting rid of the constraints around
us.

This is **the art of livin**-of self-satisfaction-
in a thread of **lineage** with our

past, **looking** forward to our future, we need
to **deal** with our present,

and **choose**.

Day 122

5:15 P.M. I was quietly eating my lettuce head and ketchup at the dinner table with Norvel, Marjorie, Michael, and Meredith, when the mint jelly came around with the lamb and I immediately passed it on. Seeing this, Norvel abruptly stood up and addressed me, "Matthew, you are a young and imma-*tur* American, and you will appreciate that *duuu*-ring your stay in Australia, with us in this household, you will learn that mint jelly goes with lamb."

"I've had mint jelly," I said. "I don't really like it. And besides, I'm not eating meat anyway."

A couple of weeks later, at the end of another extended family Saturday barbecue (no burgers this time), Marjorie called to me in the kitchen where I was washing up the dishes. "Matthew! Come here," she shouted. "Matthew! Come here." As I entered the living room, I saw the whole family—aunts, uncles, and cousins, all eighteen of them—standing in a line up against the wall. At the very end of the line was Meredith, bashfully looking down, a couple of fingers tickling her brow. Everyone was awaiting my arrival. "What's up?" I asked. Michael was on the opposite side of the room standing in a corner, nervously twiddling those fifty keys. Then Marjorie, who'd been sipping her wine all day, giddily said to me and everyone in the room, "Matthew, Meredith's about to leave, why don't you give her a kiss goodbye . . . on the lippies!"

Everyone ooh'd and ahh'd and giggled with mischief. Meredith kept her head down, five fingers now at her cheek. Michael held his clenched fists at his side and began to pace.

"I already said goodbye to Meredith, Marjorie. I gave her a hug, too," I said.

Not to be denied, Marjorie swooned, "No, no, Matthew, go on now, give her a kiss . . . on the lippies."

"What?" I said, then glanced to the end of the line at Meredith, who raised her chin just high enough to catch my eye, then quickly lowered it again.

I tried to understand what was happening. Had Meredith, over the past few months, mistaken my warmhearted humor and goodwill as romantic advances, and in doing so, formed a crush on me? Or had Marjorie just had a few too many and decided to try to pull off a tasteless prank to humiliate me, Meredith, and especially Michael? I didn't know, but either or both ways, handling it *this* way was wrong.

"My big brother" Michael was now pacing with more disgraced spite, twirling those fifty keys even faster.

Everyone else started goading me, "Yeah, do it, Matthew! Do it!"

How am I going to alleviate this situation? I thought, then took a deep breath and walked over to Meredith and calmly said to her, "Meredith, did I already give you a hug goodbye?"

Meredith, too embarrassed to look up, said nothing.

I then put two fatherly hands on her shoulders and waited until she finally raised her eyes to me.

The room had started to sober up.

"I already gave you a hug goodbye, didn't I, Meredith?"

She slowly started nodding yes.

"Thank you," I said.

"Thank *you*," she said under her breath.

Then I turned to Marjorie and sternly spoke my mind. "Marjorie, don't ever do that to me again. It is not fair. It's not fair to me, it's not fair to Meredith, it's not fair to your son Michael."

Then I walked out of the room and back to the kitchen to finish the dishes.

Damn *cultural differences*.

Day 148

I was down to 140 pounds, and my nose was constantly running.

For the last month, every night after dinner, I'd go back to my restroom, run a hot bath, listen to one of my three cassettes on my Walkman, write another fifteen-page letter to myself, and jack off to Lord Byron.

Every night.

I was now on my sixth job. I'd been a bank teller, a boat mechanic, a photo processor, a barrister's assistant, a construction worker, and an assistant golf pro.

I was sitting at the dinner table again, head down, eating my head of lettuce with ketchup, biding time until 5:45 when I could head back to the bathroom for my evening ritual, when, out of nowhere Norvel said, "Matthew, Marjorie and I have decided that for the *duur*-ation of your stay here in Australia with us, you'll refer to us as Mum and Pop."

Now, this one caught me off guard. I was speechless for a few moments as I considered how to respond.

"Thank you, Norvel," I said. "Thank you for . . . thinking of me in that way, but . . . I have a mom and a dad . . . *and* they're still alive."*

Norvel quickly snapped back, "As I said, Marjorie and I have decided that for the *duur*-ation of your stay in Australia with us, in this household, you will refer to us as Mum and Pop."

I said nothing and instead returned to finish the last of my ketchup-covered lettuce. When I was done, I politely cleared everyone's plate, took them to the kitchen, and washed them, then stopped at the dinner table to clearly address everyone before I headed back to the privacy of my evening protocol. "Good night, Nor-vel; good night, Mar-jor-ie; good night, Michael; good night, Meredith."

For the first time in 148 days, my head, heart, and spirit immediately agreed on something: *No. There is no way I'm calling anybody other than my own mom and dad "Mum and Pop." That is not negotiable. This is not a cultural difference, and if it is, then I'm not sorry, I'm just different.*

Alone in this foreign country, on my own in this uncomfortable world, I took responsibility for who I was and what I believed in. I

* Why I felt the need to contextualize my reasoning by saying "and they're still alive," as if they were not, I don't know, but I did.

made a judgment, and I chose. I did not need reassurance, and the clarity gave me identity. I was not going to lose my anchor, both on principle and in order to survive.

The next morning, my alarm clock was the sound of a shrieking woman from the other end of the house. It was 6:00 A.M.

"He! Won't! Call! Me! Mummmmm!!!! He! Won't! Call! Me! Mummmm!!!!"

I jumped out of bed and ran to find Marjorie, bawling her eyes out, puddles of tears on the table, shrieking to the heavens.

I put my arm around her. "C'mon, Marjorie, it's not personal. How would you feel if your son, Michael, called someone else Mum and Pop?"

We had a good cry together, for different reasons.

That's when I decided that maybe it was time for me to find another family to live with for the *duur*-ation of my stay.

That afternoon there was a tornado. There wasn't a car on the street. It was raining sideways, 45 mph winds, the sky was deep pink and yellow. I went on my daily run anyway, all the way to the house of the president of the local Rotary Club, Harris Stewart.

He answered the door. "Mate, what are you bloody hell doing? What's goin on?"

"I'm just out for a run, Harris, want to see you about something."

"Well, get your ass inside, we're under a tornado warning, and you're out for a jog?"

I stepped in and toweled off.

"What's up, mate?" he asked.

I took a deep breath. "Listen, man, if it's possible, I was wondering if there's another family in the Rotary Club that could take me in?"

"Everything all right over at the Dooleys'?"

"Yeah, yeah, everything's fine," I said, not wanting to be a tattletale. "I just want to experience . . . another family if I can."

"For a family to take you in, it means feeding another mouth, Matthew," he said, "and the economy hasn't been so good around here for a while, but . . . I'll see what I can do."

God bless Harris Stewart.

He reached out to Connor Harrington, my friend who managed the bank I'd worked at as a teller. Connor and his wife agreed to take me in. God bless Connor Harrington. That Thursday, at the weekly Rotary meeting, Harris Stewart declared, over the microphone, to the entire room, that, "Our exchange student, Matthew, has been happily living with the Dooleys for the past six months—thank you, Norvel." Big applause. "And he is now going to be moving in with the Harringtons— thank you, Connor." More applause.

The meeting adjourned, there were glad hands all around.

It was all wrapped up, no drama. Norvel Dooley was right there in the meeting, sitting next to me during Harris's announcement. Now he was shaking hands in agreement, singing my praises to the rest of the Rotary members, fully aware of, and in accordance with, the new plan. "I'll be by to pick you up this coming Tuesday at 6:30 P.M.," Connor said to me in front of Norvel. "Fair dinkum,* Connor, we'll see you then," Norvel replied. Great, all set.

Norvel and I rode home together—he said nothing to me.

That night I said "good night" to Norvel and Marjorie before bed, they said "good night" back, nothing more. The next morning, I woke up, had breakfast, went to work, came home, had dinner, and said "good night" again before bed. Nothing.

Saturday came—there was no family over for a goodbye party, no *what are we gonna do on your last days here* . . . nothing.

Sunday—nothing.

Monday—nothing.

Tuesday morning—nothing.

* *Fair dinkum* is an Aussie slang meaning *for sure, absolutely, without a doubt.*

I came home from work early, my two suitcases having been packed since last Thursday night, and triple-checked that I had everything ready to go.

Five days had passed with not one word of acknowledgment of my leaving when we sat down at the dinner table to have our final 5:00 P.M. supper together—me, Norvel, Marjorie, Michael, and Meredith. I chomped on my lettuce head with ketchup. They ate in silence.

At 5:30 I got up from the table and went to wash the dishes. Nothing.

When I was done, I walked back to my room to quadruple-check that I had everything packed. Connor was going to be here in less than thirty minutes. He couldn't come soon enough. I paced my bedroom floor, checking my watch every thirty seconds.

Then I heard a knock on my door.

I opened it.

And there in the doorway stood Norvel Dooley, hands on his hips, legs slightly apart, in a sturdy squared-up stance.

"Hey, Norvel. What's up?"

Without flinching, he said, "Matthew, Marjorie and I have decided that you will be staying with us for the *duur*-ation of your stay in Australia, in this household, with us. Unpack your bags."

In the twilight of my Twilight Zone, shocked, I rallied and took the high road once again.

"Uhh . . . thank you, Norvel, for offering your home to me for the rest of my stay here in Australia," I said, trying to remain calm. "But I have a full year here in your country, in Warnervale, and I want to experience as much as possible, and . . . livin with a different family will be another experience for me."

He raised his chin and settled his heels into the floor. "Matthew, unpack your bags. Marjorie and I have decided that you'll be staying with us for the *duur*-ation of your stay here in Australia," he repeated.

I lost it. I reared back and sent a vicious left hook through the bedroom door so forceful that my fist came out the other side. I pulled my arm out, bloody and pierced from shards of plywood. I was shaking, full of rage, confused again. Norvel started to shake as well, his eyes bulging in shock.

"Norvel," I growled, "you get your fat fucking ass out of my way or I am going to beat you to the ground and drag you across your gravel driveway for so long that you are gonna be pullin rocks outta your back until the day you fucking DIE!"

He started twitching, his mouth began to tremble and drop open, then he began to back up.

I stood there, staring him down, fists clenched, with a bloody arm, about to piss my pants I was so livid.

That's when he turned around and walked away.

I removed the splinters from my arm and washed it in the bathroom sink. I soaked a towel with cold water and wiped my arm and face. I paced the room trying to bring my heart rate down and figure out what the fuck had just gone down, when I heard the sound of a car horn. I looked at my watch. It was 6:30.

I rolled my bags down the hallway, past Norvel's office, across the living room, through the kitchen, and out the garage to the driveway. There was Connor Harrington in his Land Cruiser. Norvel was there, too, along with Marjorie, Michael, and Meredith—everybody—hugging and carrying on like they were sending their last son off to join the army overseas. Marjorie wept on her walker. Michael was crying like a baby as he gave me a bear hug. Meredith sobbed and tickled her cheeks as I kissed her on the forehead. Even Norvel dried a tear. They loaded my suitcases in the back of the Land Cruiser and Connor and I drove away. In the rearview mirror the Dooleys were lined up at the top of the driveway, standing in the very place where I had stood when I first arrived, arms around each other, shedding tears and waving goodbye until I was out of sight.

Day 326

It was a Saturday night, and my last in Australia. The next day I'd be boarding a plane home. I'd been there one day short of a calendar year.

Now livin* with the Stewarts for the last few months, I'd stayed with a family called the Travers for the two before that, and the Harringtons the one prior. All of them were outstanding people and also best of friends with one another. Tonight, they were all gathered at Harris's house for my farewell party. We were doing what we always did on Saturday nights—Harris played guitar while we all took turns reading Woody Allen's *Side Effects* out loud, laughing our asses off, drinking port wine until three in the morning.

It was just past midnight when Connor Harrington blurted out of nowhere, "Hey, Macka (his Aussie nickname for me), how in the bloody hell did you live with the Dooleys for that long?"

Partially stunned, I asked, "What do you mean?"

The whole room broke out into belly laughs, a cacophony of hysteria.

My mouth dropped, I looked around at each one of them, dumbfounded. They were curled over with laughter, thought it was hilarious. Finally I cried out, "You motherfuckers! You let me stay there!? I almost lost my mind!" They laughed even harder. Then I began to laugh, and soon we were *all* rolling on the floor.

It was a big Australian prank.

As eccentric as the Dooleys were, they were a kind family at heart and generous in offering me a home. But the time I spent there *was* torturous for me. A livin mental hell. A true red light at the time. All my visions of grandeur were a mirage.

But a "handshake deal" never gave me the option of returning home, so I endured. Only later did I come to realize that the suffering and loneliness I experienced would be one of the most important sacrifices of my life.

Before my trip to Australia I was never an introspective man. On that trip I was forced to look inside myself for the first time to make

* You'll understand later why I never put a "g" on the end of "livin."

sense of what was going on around me.

The life I had left back home in Texas was summertime year-round. "Most handsome," straight A's, dating the best-looking girl at my school (*and* across town), a truck that was paid for, and I. Had. No. Curfew.

Australia, the land of sunny beaches, bikinis, and surfboards I never saw, gave me the ability to respect winter. I was on my own, for a full year. I was in the bathtub every night before sundown jacking off to Lord Byron and *Rattle and Hum*. Telling myself daily, *I'm okay, I'm good. You got this McConaughey, it's just* cultural differences. I was a vegetarian, down to 130 pounds, abstinent, planning to become a monk and free Nelson Mandela.

Yeah, I was forced into a winter. Forced to look inside myself because I didn't have anyone else. I didn't have any*thing* else. I'd lost my crutches. No mom and dad, no friends, no girlfriend, no straight A's, no phone, no truck, no "Most Handsome."

And I had a curfew.

It was a year that shaped who I am today.

A year when I found myself because I was forced to.

A year that also planted the seeds of a notion that continues to guide me: Life's hard. Shit happens to us. We make shit happen. To me, it was **inevitable** that I was staying the entire year because I'd shaken on it. I'd made a voluntary obligation with myself that there was "no goin back." So I got **relative**. I denied the reality that the Dooleys *were not like anyone I had met before*. It *was* a crisis for me. I just didn't give the crisis credit. I treaded water until I crossed the finish line. I persisted. I upheld my father's integrity.

And while I was going crazy, I kept telling myself that there was a lesson I was put there to learn, that there was a silver lining in all of it, that I needed to go through hell to get to the other side, and I did. We cannot fully appreciate the light without the shadows. We have to be thrown *off* balance to find our footing. It's better to jump than fall. And here I am.

GREENLIGHT.

P.S. The Dooleys' son Rhys was also in the exchange program, and he came over to live at my house with my parents while I was with his. What kind of time did he have?

My parents took him to NASA, to Six Flags, and to Florida for the summer, where he threw parties every weekend. Clearly taking advantage of his accent, he took an ex-girlfriend of mine on dates in my truck, and I was told that his seed was distributed freely. The liquor cabinet was drained. He had the time of his fucking life.

```
the monster

The future is the          The dragon not yet
monster                    tamed.

not the boogeyman          On a one-way
under the bed.             collision course
                           with no turning
The past is just           back,
something we're
trying to outrun           the future, the
tomorrow.                  monster,

The monster is the         is always waiting
future.                    for us and

The unknown.               always sees us
                           a-comin.
The boundaries not
yet crossed.               so we should lift
                           our heads,
The challenge not
yet met.                   look it in the eye,

The potential not          and watch it heed.
yet realized.
```

Back home in Texas, I was nineteen years old, had a year in Australia under my belt, and was now *drinking age*. On the way home from buying dog food and paper towels at Walmart one night, Dad and I stopped by a neon-lit pool hall in a strip mall on the southwest side of Houston.

We had a few beers, I met a few of his friends, mostly kept to my *yes* and *no sirs*, but had enough confidence and experience to chime in to some of the tall tale telling. A couple hours later we paid the tab at the bar and started to leave. As I stepped out of the entrance door, my dad behind me, the big-bicepped bouncer who was standing just outside stepped in front of my dad and said, "You pay your bill?"

Without slowing his pace, Dad said, "Sure did, pal," and continued walking. That's when the man at the door did something that my mind's eye can still see in slow motion today. In an attempt to slow my dad's passage, *he put his hand on my dad's chest.* Another man's hand on *my* dad. Before Dad could correct this wannabe muscleman with his own hands, I did with mine.

The next thing I remember: I was on top of this bouncer who was now splayed across a table fifteen feet back *inside* the bar. I pounded down on him with vicious right fists until the drunken jeers of a good bar fight slowly turned to murmurs. The fight was over. It had *been* over, but not for me. Then I felt myself being pulled off the man and held back. I continued to kick and spit at the doorman on the floor until I heard a strong, calming voice in my ear, "That's enough, son, that's enough."

That night was *my* rite of passage. Dad let me in. It was the night I became *his boy, a man* in his eyes. The night we became friends. The night he called every one of his buddies who knew me and said, "The youngest one's gonna be okay, boys, you shoulda seen him take this big ol' boy out last night at the bar, just decked him . . . We gotta keep an eye on him, though, he's got a berserker switch, he's a little bit crazy."

From that night on I could go to the bar with him, my brother Mike, and all the men I'd been calling *Mr.* all my life. It was a primitive initiation into my father's regard, but finally, instead of only *hearing* about the stories from last night the next day, I could be a *part* of them.

GREENLIGHT.

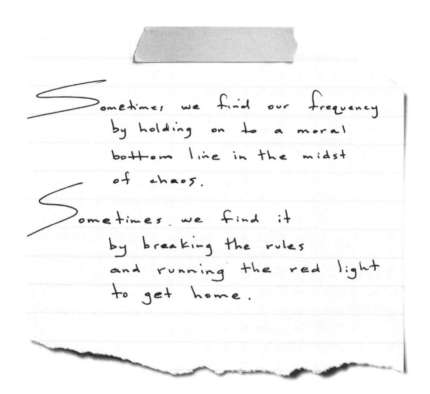

Sometimes we find our frequency
by holding on to a moral
bottom line in the midst
of chaos.
Sometimes we find it
by breaking the rules
and running the red light
to get home.

66Style is knowing who you
are, what you want to say,
and not giving a damn.**99**

Gore Vidal (1925–)

- 5-8-89 -

"A   Isn't that the fuck'in truth. To have style
you have to have these in this order. You've got to
know who you are before you know what you want
to say then not give a damn. But knowing who
you are is the base that everthing else comes from.
I've got more style now than ever before
but I'm still adding to my style. You know
who you are when you became independent
enough to believe your own thoughts and became
responsible for your actions and you not
only "believe" what you want but you
<u>live what you believe</u>. LIVE WHAT YOU
BELIEVE... "LIVE THE QUESTIONS FIRST,
THEN WHAT YOU BELIEVE (slight changes)...
THEN YOU HAVE YOUR OWN PERSONAL

STYLE"......

mom.
That was fun to write

DIRT ROADS
AND
AUTOBAHNS

WHILE IN AUSTRALIA I HAD begun applying to colleges. Duke, Grambling, UT Austin, and Southern Methodist. I wanted to study law and become a defense attorney. That had been the plan since ninth grade. I was a great debater and the somewhat serious joke in my household was "Matthew's gonna become our lawyer, defend the family business, prosecute some bigwigs, make us some 'Oil of Mink' money."

I was set on SMU, largely because it was in the metropolitan city of Dallas, and I believed Dallas would have more opportunities for me to intern in a law firm, which would then give me a better chance of having a job as soon as I graduated.

One night Dad called me. "Son, you sure you don't wanna be a Longhorn?" (My dad always named a school after its mascot and was particularly fond of UT's.)

"No, Dad, I wanna be a Mustang (SMU's mascot), I'm pretty sure about it."

He grumbled.

"Is that all right with you, Dad?"

"Oh, sure, son, sure, just thought you might wanna consider being a Longhorn is all."

"No sir, I wanna be a Mustang."

"Okay, that'll work," he said and we hung up.

An hour later my brother Pat called.

"What's up?" I asked.

"You sure you don't wanna be a Texas Longhorn, little brother?"

"Yeah, big brother."

"You sure?"

"Yeah, I'm sure, why do you and Dad keep asking me that?"

"Well, Dad won't ever tell ya, but the oil business is in bad shape. He's broke, tryin to keep from goin Chapter 11." (The oil boom that had moved us from Uvalde to Longview in '79 had dried up, and it turned out Dad had been hustling to pay the bills for the last few years.)

"He is?"

"Yep, and it'll cost eighteen thousand a year to go SMU cus it's private, but only five a year to go to UT cus it's public."

"Oh shit, I had no idea."

"Yeah, and, little brother, you ever been to Austin?"

"No."

"You're gonna love it, buddy, it is your kinda town. You can walk into anywhere in your flip-flops, have a seat at a bar, and you'll have a cowboy to the right of you, a lesbian to your left, an Indian on the other side, and a midget tendin bar. All you gotta be is yourself in that town."

I called Dad back the next day. "I changed my mind, I wanna be a Longhorn."

"You do?" he said, not masking his excitement.

"Yes, sir."

"Oh, gawdammy, little buddy, great choice! What made you change your mind?"

"I just like Longhorns better than Mustangs."

Out of respect for my dad, I attended the University of Texas at

Austin but never told him why. I knew changing my mind would make Dad happy. I'd soon change it again, but this time I wasn't so sure of his reaction.

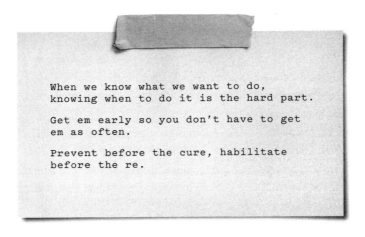

When we know what we want to do,
knowing when to do it is the hard part.

Get em early so you don't have to get
em as often.

Prevent before the cure, habilitate
before the re.

It was the end of my sophomore year in college, final exams were looming, and I wasn't sleeping well. Not because of my mattress, because of my mind. I was having doubts about my plans to become a lawyer. The math didn't add up. Four years of undergrad and I'd be twenty-three, then three more at law school and I'd be twenty-six before I'd get out, get a job. I wouldn't start making my mark in this world until I was almost thirty years old. I didn't want to miss my twenties preparing for the rest of my life.

I'd also been writing short stories in my journal. I passed a few off to my good friend Robb Bindler, a film student at NYU, who attested they were original and worth sharing. "Thought about film school?" he asked. "You're a good storyteller." Film school? That sounded so flattering, but it also sounded so foreign, almost European, radical, irresponsible, indulgent—so "artsy." I couldn't even get the idea into the dialect of my dreams, much less consider it as a rational aspiration. Nah, not for me.

A few hours before my psychology final exam, I showed up at my fraternity, grabbed lunch, and went across the back alley to a couple of fellow Delt brothers' place so I could finish studying. They were both sleeping in bunk beds because they'd pulled all-nighters cramming. I sat on their couch and opened my textbook. I was a diligent studier. I would use every spare second I had to prepare for a test and took great pride in being composed and ready for any exam. I made a lot of A's.

But on this day, for some reason, with the exam only a few hours away, I said to myself, *You've got this McConaughey,* and put the textbook and my notes back in my backpack and turned on the TV. ESPN. Now, I love sports. I will watch the World's Strongest Man competition if that's all that's on. Today it was a baseball game. Even better. But after five minutes, for some reason, I shut the TV off, not interested.

I looked around the room. On the floor to the left of me was a stack of magazines. *Playboys, Hustlers.* Now, I love women, and I love looking at naked women. But for some reason, not today. Not interested. As I flipped about seven mags deep into the pile I came across a small paperback book. It had a white cover with a handsome red cursivelike title. It read:

The Greatest Salesman in the World

Who's that? I wondered as I picked it up from the pile and began to read.

Two and a half hours later I got to the first "Scroll" in the book. The book had just revealed that the title was referring to the reader of the book, *me,* in this instance, and now my instructions were to read each scroll three times a day for thirty days before moving on to the next one. I looked at my watch. My exam was in twenty minutes.

I rustled my friend from his bunk. "Can I borrow this book, Braedon?" I asked.

"No, man, you can have it."

I left, book in hand, and made it to my test on time.

I was high. Something about this book, the title, the story so far, the mystery of the ten scrolls, felt special, like *it* had found *me.*

I rushed through my exam. I didn't care about psychology class and I didn't care what grade I made, I only cared about reading that first scroll. Somehow I knew that something bigger than a classroom exam lay within the pages of this book.

SCROLL 1

"I will form good habits and
become their slave."

It occurred to me that it was a bad habit to lie to myself any longer. Becoming a lawyer wasn't for me. I wanted to tell stories. I paced my dorm room trying to assess the best time to call my dad and tell him I had changed my mind and no longer wanted to go to law school, I wanted to go to film school. At 7:30, I thought, he would just have had dinner and would be relaxing on the couch with his first cocktail, catching some tube with Mom. Yeah, 7:30 was the right time to call.

My dad taught us to do a job well and climb the nine-to-five company ladder. I had been groomed to be the family's lawyer. We were a blue-collar family. Film school? Oh shit.

Taking deep breaths, sweating, I made the call at 7:36 P.M.

Dad answered.

"Hey, Pop," I said.

"Hey, little buddy, what's goin on?" he asked.

Another deep breath. "Well, I wanna share something with you."

"What's that?"

Oh shit.

"Well, I don't want to go to law school anymore, I want to go to film school."

Silence. One. Two. Three. Four. Five seconds.

Then I heard a voice. A kind, inquisitive voice.

"Is that what you wanna do?" he asked.

"Yes sir, Dad, it is."

Silence. Another five seconds.

"Well . . . **Don't half-ass it.**"

Of all the things my dad could have said, of all the reactions he could have had, *Don't half-ass it* were the last words I expected to hear and the best words he could have ever said to me. With those words he not only gave me his blessing and consent, he gave me his approval and validation. It's what he said and *how* he said it. He not only gave me privilege, he gave me honor, freedom, and responsibility. With some formidable rocket fuel in his delivery, we made a pact that day. Thanks, Pop.

GREENLIGHT.

```
biology and giddyup

DNA and work.

Genetics and willpower.

Life's a combination.

Some get the genes but never the
work ethic or resilience.

Others work their ass off but never
had the innate ability.

Others have both and never rely on
the first.
```

I didn't have a short film or a piece of art to audition for film school, but I had a 3.82 GPA. Not only did it get me into film school, it got me into the Honors Program.

But now I was pursuing a career path, where, unlike law, my GPA did not matter. I knew Hollywood and artists didn't care if I made A's or F's, they needed to *see* something worthy of their attention. I needed to *make* something—a film, a performance. I needed a job.

I signed with the local Donna Adams Talent Agency and started interning at an ad agency four days a week between classes. I wore a pager on my hip and would step out of class without hesitation to drive to San Antonio or Dallas to audition for a music video or a beer ad. I got a bunch of no-thank-yous.

The first gig I landed was as a hand model. Donna Adams had told me upon signing that I had "good-lookin hands," and if I "quit biting my nails" I might have a future in the hand modeling business. She was correct. I've never bit my nails since.

Good looks don't cook the dinner, but they'll get you a seat at the table, and I was determined to take advantage of any seat I could get. I directed short films in black-and-white on 16 mm Bolex cameras, I edited, I assistant directed other classmates' films, I directed photography, I wrote and performed. I missed a lot of classes driving to San Antonio and Dallas.

One day, the dean called me into his office. "Matthew, attendance is mandatory in our classes, especially the Honors Program. You cannot keep missing class or leaving in the middle of class as you have been. If you continue to do so, I will have to fail you."

"Dean," I said, looking him directly in the eye, "you and I both know that a degree in film production doesn't mean squat to studio heads in Hollywood and New York City. It means nothing to the people that make movies. They want to see a product. A film, a performance, something. The only reason I'm skipping class is to go out into the world and try and make something that those people will want to purchase. I'm chasing things outside of the classroom that the classroom is teaching me to chase." Then I had an idea, and I blurted it out. "If I promise to make it to every exam day in class, will you just gimme C's across the board?"

He didn't answer.

Nonetheless, I stuck to my proposal. I kept skipping classes to chase my pager and I made sure I showed up as prepared as possible on exam days.

At the end of the semester, I received a C in every class on my college transcript. But I learned a lot more than when I was making A's.

GREENLIGHT.

I'LL TAKE A LITTLE COMMON SENSE WITH THAT KNOWLEDGE

I was an outcast in class anyway. The only frat guy in film school. Boots. Pressed button-down. Tucked in. Tan. Affable. Nonneurotic.

Most everyone else wore black. They were pale, goth, and huddled in their private corners.

One of our professors made us go see movies each weekend and come back on Monday and talk about them with the class. I would always go to the Metroplex and see the blockbuster, then come in on Monday and say, "Hey, I saw *Die Hard* this weekend and . . ."

"Nah, that's shit, man, that's shit, it sucks," my classmates would say before I could finish my sentence. They had all gone and seen the Eisenstein revival.

I began to doubt myself. "This is what you have to do to be an artist, McConaughey. You have to see the art films at the art house, not the blockbusters at the Metroplex. You aren't independent enough, you need to be more eccentric, less friendly." I started untucking my shirt.

But I still went to see the blockbusters. The next Monday I got in front of the class to talk about what I'd seen, and again, the rest of the students started murmuring, "That's big studio *shit,* man . . . corporate America sellouts."

This time I said, "Wait a minute. Tell me why it's *shit*. Why it sucks. What you didn't like about it."

They all got quiet, heads started looking to each other. Finally, one of them said, "Well . . . we didn't actually *see* it. We just *know* it's shit."

"Fuck y'all," I said. "Fuck y'all for saying something is shit just because it's popular!"

After that day I was comfortable being both in the fraternity and a film student.

I tucked my shirt back in.

Fascinated with the differences between people and cultures, I've always enjoyed looking for and finding the common denominator of values that are the foundation beneath our distinctions. When my college buddies and I would hit Sixth Street for a night out, they'd go to the popular bars littered with sorority girl possibilities and I'd go to Catfish Station, an all-black, sweaty bar that sold catfish, beer, and blues. It was standing room only when Kyle Turner was on his saxophone or the all-blind band Blue Mist were on the stage. I'd find my spot stage left by the beer cooler. I'd lean against it, serve myself, and let the cool air keep my perspiration from dripping. Laron managed the joint. Tammy was the black-and-beautiful-as-midnight rock star waitress who ran the floor and had every single dude in the joint thinking they had a chance

TRIBES

We want lovers, friends, recruits, soldiers, and affiliations that support who we are.

People, individuals, believe in themselves, want to survive, and on a Darwinistic level at least, want to have more, of ourselves.

Initially, this is a visual choice.

The where, what, when, and who . . . to our why.

Upon closer inspection, which is the upfall of the politically correct culture of today, we learn to measure people on the competence of *their* values that *we* most value.

When we do this, the politics of gender, race, and slanderous slang take a back seat to the importance of the values we share.

The more we travel, the more we realize how similar our human needs are.

We want to be loved, have a family, community, have something to look forward to.

These basic needs are present in all socioeconomic and cultural civilizations.

I have seen many tribes in the deserts of Northern Africa who, with nine children and no electricity, had more joy, love, honor, and laughter than the majority of the most materially rich people I've ever met.

We have the choice to love, befriend, recruit, call to arms, associate, and support

who we believe in, and more importantly, who, we believe, believes in us.

I think that's what we all want. To believe in and be believed in.

We all must earn belief in ourselves first, then for each other.

Earn it with you, then earn it with me, *then* we earn it for we.

Travel and humanity have been my greatest educators.

They have helped me understand the common denominator of mankind. Values.

Engage with yourself then engage with the world.

Values travel.

And sometimes we get a stamp in our passport just by crossing the street.

just so they'd tip more. None of them did—have a chance, that is—me included, but we tipped a little extra anyway. One night around closing time while paying Laron for the six bottles of beer I'd drunk, I told him I wanted a job waiting tables. The hand modeling gigs were sparse and I needed some extra spending money, and besides, I liked the blues. Laron laughed. I was the only white person, male or female, who was ever in the place.

"I'm serious, I need the cash and I like the music in here," I said.

He laughed again, then stared at me a minute.

"Ahh-ight, you crazy motherfucker," he said, pulling out a pen and writing on a receipt. "Go to this address Tuesday morning at nine and ask for Homer. He's the owner. I'll let him know you're comin."

I showed up at the appointed time. The place was also on Sixth Street but in a much bigger, open-floored club. Business at Catfish Station was good, and the joint would soon be moving up to a larger venue—this one. In the middle of the room stood a black man, well over 340 pounds, wearing an all-white janitor's uniform and dripping sweat on the concrete floor he was mopping. Another black man was standing at the bar, back to the entrance, doing paperwork.

"Homer?" I asked aloud.

The man at the bar didn't move. The other guy kept mopping.

"Homer Hill!" I said a bit louder.

The man at the bar turned his head over his right shoulder like he'd been interrupted.

"Yeah, that's me."

"I'm Matthew, Laron told me to come by here and see you. I wanna be a waiter at Catfish Station."

Over his shoulder he said, "Oh yeah, that's right; grab a mop and go with Carl to clean the men's room."

Carl turned with his mop and began rolling his water bucket back toward the bathrooms. Never turning back, he pointed at another mop and bucket against the back wall.

Not what I was expecting. I smiled. Homer did not. So I stepped to it, went to the men's room, and started mopping the floors like I was trying to take Carl's job.

Ten to fifteen minutes passed. Head down, cleaning a stall, I heard, "Man, put that mop down."

I turned and there was Homer.

"You really want a job waitin tables?"

"Yeah, I do," I said.

Homer shook his head a bit and let out a breathy giggle. "All right, show up at the Station, Thursday night at six P.M. You can shadow Tammy and learn the ropes."

On Thursday night I showed up at Catfish Station at 5:45. I knew Tammy from the many nights I'd been a customer, but now I was there to learn from her and she was not too happy about it. Tammy was the queen bee—she ran the entire floor—and I was now trespassing on her territory, and her tips. But for the next three nights, Tammy initiated me. Where to clock in for work, how to run the register, how to place orders with the cooks, what to tip them at the end of the night, which tables would soon be mine, and which high-tipping customers I best not even look at.

The next Thursday night I started waiting tables for real. Game on. The clientele was 90 percent black men, 10 percent black women *with* those black men. Eighty percent of those black men were single and as much as they liked the blues, they came to the Station for Tammy. And they weren't delighted to be waited on by a young white man, and their tips told me as much. At the end of night one, I cleared $32. Tammy made $98.

I waited tables at Catfish Station Thursday through Saturday for the next two years. Many of those black men became my friends and even came to *choose* my section. Many, not most. Tammy and I became pretty close but, like every other straight man in the Station, she never let me get so much as a peck on the cheek. I never stopped trying. I never beat her in tips, either.

Homer and I have maintained a friendship through the years. We went to a Longhorn game together last season.

GREENLIGHT.

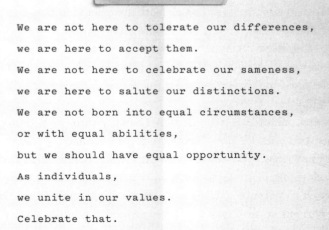

We are not here to tolerate our differences,
we are here to accept them.
We are not here to celebrate our sameness,
we are here to salute our distinctions.
We are not born into equal circumstances,
or with equal abilities,
but we should have equal opportunity.
As individuals,
we unite in our values.
Celebrate that.

I had a little cash in my pocket from my job at Catfish Station, but not so much that I didn't appreciate a free drink. I picked up my girlfriend, Tonia, and took her to the bar at the top of the Hyatt where my classmate Sam was bartending, hence the free drinks.

"Two vodka and tonics, Sam."

He brought them over and said, "There's a guy at the end of the bar who's in town producing a movie. He's been comin in here nightly. Lemme introduce you to him."

This is when I met the one and only Don Phillips.

I welcomed him to Austin. We were both golfers and had played some of the same courses. He drank vodka and tonics as well, many of them.

A few hours later, as Don stood atop a chair in the midst of delivering one of his legendarily loud charades of a story, the management, to no avail, tried to calm him down. When it was obvious Don wanted nothing to do with toning *anything* down, they tried to kick him out of the bar.

Matching him drink for drink, I had no interest in Don calming down either, so we were unpeacefully escorted out of the Hyatt. Now past two in the morning, as he rode with me in a cab to drop me off at my apartment, I pulled out a joint and we smoked it.

"You ever done any acting, Matthew?" he asked.

I told him I'd been in a Miller Lite commercial for about a second and a half and had done a music video for Trisha Yearwood.

"Well, there's a small part in this movie I'm casting you might be right for. Come to this address tomorrow morning at nine thirty and pick up the script, I'll have the three scenes marked."

The cabbie dropped me off at my apartment and Don and I said our good nights.

The next morning at 9:30 (really the same morning just six hours later) I arrived at the location Don had given me and there was a script with my name on it, and a handwritten note from Don that read, "Here's the script, the character's name is 'Wooderson,' I'll get you in for an audition in two weeks."

Over the years I've come to call the kind of line in a script that can send me flying a "launchpad" line. This script was for *Dazed and Confused*. The line that sent me into flight was:

"That's what I love about these high school girls, man.
I get older, they stay the same age."

Wooderson was twenty-two years old but still hanging out around the high school. That line opened up an entire world into who he was, an encyclopedia into his psyche and spirit. I thought about my brother Pat when he was a senior, and I was eleven. He was my big brother, my hero. One day, Pat's Z28 was in the shop so Mom and I were picking him up from high school.

We were slowly pulling through campus in our '77 wood-paneled station wagon, Mom driving, me peering out the window in the back seat. Pat was not where we had planned to meet him.

"Where is he?" asked Mom.

Turning my head to look left and right and then out the back window, I saw him about a hundred yards behind us, leaning against the brick wall in the shade of the school's smoking section, one knee bent, boot sole against the side of the building, pulling on a Marlboro, cooler than James Dean and two feet taller.

"Ther—!!" I started to shriek, then caught my tongue because I realized he'd get in trouble for smoking.

"What's that?" Mom asked.

"Nothin, Mom, nothin."

That image of my big brother, leaning against *that* wall, casually smoking *that* cigarette in his low-elbow, loose-wristed, lazy-fingered way, through my romantic eleven-year-old little brother eyes, was

105

the epitome of cool. He was literally ten feet tall. It left an engraved impression in my heart and mind.

And eleven years later, Wooderson was born from *that* impression.

```
                                       cool

                    cool is a natural law.

                if it was cool for THAT time,

                then it is cool for ALL time.

        a fad is just a branch on cool's trunk,

          a fashionable fling whose 15 minutes
                             can never abide,

        no matter how long she trends to try.

                cool stands the test of time.

                    because cool never tries.

                           cool just is.
```

I had ten days to prepare for the audition and I knew *my man*. But, being that this was technically a job interview, I made sure to shave and tuck in my best long-sleeve button-down. When I got there and met the director, Richard Linklater, he soon said, "You're not really this guy, are you?"

"No," I said, "but I know who he is," then I leaned back, lowered my eyelids, held my cigarette between the peace sign, and gave him my Wooderson.

I got the job.

He told me not to shave.

Production was already in full swing. Soon I got called to set to do a "makeup and wardrobe" test, meaning, I would go through makeup and hair in the trailer that was already on set for the working actors, then I would get into my selected wardrobe, then Rick would come by during a break from shooting to approve or make comments on my overall "look."

They were shooting at the Top Notch hamburger drive-in that night. I remember stepping out of the makeup trailer, in full wardrobe, onto the sidewalk off Burnet Road in North Austin about thirty yards from set. Rick came over. On approach, he began to smile widely as he took me in. He spread his arms in his open-palmed way as he looked me up and down.

"Peach pants . . . the Nuge T-shirt . . . the comb-over . . . the 'stache . . . Is that a black panther tattoo on your forearm?"

"Yeah, man, whaddaya think?"

"I dig it. This is great, this is Wooderson."

Now remember, I wasn't there to act that night. Wooderson wasn't in any of the scenes that were being shot. I was only there for Rick to approve my hair, makeup, and wardrobe.

That's when Rick got an idea, and we began to do something that to this day we still do, which is play a game of "verbal ping-pong."

"I know Wooderson has probably been with the typical 'hot' high school chicks," he said, "cheerleaders, majorettes, girls like that—but you think he'd have any interest in the redheaded intellectual?"

"Sure, man, Wooderson likes all kinds of chicks."

"Yeah, right? . . . Ya know, Marissa Ribisi is playing Cynthia, the redheaded intellectual girl, and she's over here at the drive-in with her nerdy friends in the back seat. You think Wooderson might pull up and try and pick her up?"

"Gimme thirty minutes."

I took a walk with myself.

Who's my man? I asked myself. *What's goin on tonight in this scene?*

It's their last day of school, everyone's lookin for the party. I'd know some Spanish.

Next thing I know I'm in my car (well, Wooderson's car) on set, mic'd up.

"So on action, you just pull up next to her car like Wooderson would and try and pick her up," Rick instructed.

"Cool, got it."

Now, there were no lines written and this was my first time on a film set. I'd never done this before. Anxious, I started going back over in my head *who* my man *is.*

Who's my man? Who's Wooderson? What do I love?

I love my car.

Well, I'm in my '70 Chevelle. That's one.

I love getting high.

Well, Slater's riding shotgun and he's always got a doobie rolled up. That's two.

I love rock 'n' roll. Well, I've got Nugent's "Stranglehold" in the 8-track. That's three.

That's when I heard, "Action!"

I looked up across the parking lot at "Cynthia," the redheaded intellectual, and said to myself, *And I love chicks.*

As I put the car in drive and slowly pulled out, I thought to myself, *Well, I've got three out of four and I'm headed to get the fourth,* then said aloud,

```
alright,

alright,

alright
```

Those three words, those three affirmations of *what* I, Wooderson, *did* have, were the first three words I ever said on film. A film that my character had only three scripted scenes in, a film that I ended up working on for three weeks.

Now, twenty-eight years later, those words follow me everywhere. People say them. People steal them. People wear them on their hats and T-shirts. People have them tattooed on their arms and inner thighs. And I love it. It's an honor. Because those three words are the very first words I said on the very first night of a job I had that I thought might be nothing but a hobby, but turned into a career.

GREENLIGHT.

oneinarow

Any success takes one in a row.

Do one thing well, then another.

Once, then once more.

Over and over until the end,

then it's oneinarow again.

Five days into shooting, I got a call from my mom at about seven o'clock in the evening. I was in the kitchen.

"Your dad died."

My knees buckled. I couldn't believe it. My dad was the abominable snowman, the immovable force, a bear of a man, with the immune system of a Viking and the strength of a bull. Impossible. He was my dad. Nobody or no thing could kill him.

Except Mom.

He'd always told me and my brothers, "Boys, when I go, I'm gonna be makin love to your mother."

And that's what happened.

When he woke up that morning at 6:30, feeling frisky, he made love to the woman he had divorced twice, and married three times. His wife, *Kay*, my mom.

He had a heart attack when he climaxed.

Yes, he called his shot all right.

110

Days of Prosperity

Days of prosperity
make us forget
adversity.

Good times seem out
of reach during the
bad ones.

Both can seem like
final destinations,

the summation of our
days.

Then the cosmic
joker plays with our
ways,

Yesterday's
condition no longer
remains,

All commas, no
periods, all stops,
no stays,

the pleasure's for
rent and so is the
pain.

I drove home to Houston that night. We had an Irish wake two days later where hundreds of friends gathered and told stories about him, just the way he'd instructed us to when he talked about his passing.

Losing my father, like it is for many, was my most seminal rite of passage into manhood. No more safety net. No one above the law and government looking after me anymore. It was time for me to grow up. Time to say goodbye to the boy I'd been, building tree houses in the middle of the night.

A realization came to me. I carved these words into a tree:

less impressed,

more involved.

The sooner we become *less impressed* with our life, our accomplishments, our career, our relationships, the prospects in front of us—the

man enuf

man enuf

man enuf to admit I'm
scared

man enuf to know it

just man enuf

man enuf to man up

man enuf to be a man

man enuf to be me

just man enuf

man enuf to feel love

man enuf to know love

man enuf to love

just man enuf

man enuf to want to be
there

man enuf to be on my
way

man enuf to be in a
traffic jam and know I
need a road trip

just man enuf

man enuf to be drunk
and sober

man enuf to be sober
and drunk

man enuf to get outta
the trance to enter
the dream

just man enuf

man enuf to lead

man enuf to follow

man enuf to lie beside

man enuf to sleep
alone

just man enuf

man enuf to die for
life

man enuf to live for
death

just man enuf

man enuf to have
heroes

man enuf to become my
own

just man enuf

man enuf not to know

man enuf to find out

just man enuf

man enuf to apologize

man enuf to realize

just man enuf

sooner we become less impressed and *more involved* with these things—the sooner we get better at them. We must be more than just happy to be here.

All the mortal things that I had been *revering* in my life, everything I was looking *up* to in awe, suddenly came *down* to *eye level* in front of me. All the mortal things that I looked down upon and patronized in my life, suddenly rose *up* to eye level.

Now, the world was flat, and I was looking it *in* the eye.

It was time to trade in *any* red sport cars I still had.

It was time to stop dreaming and start dealing.

It was time for me to take care of Mom.

It was time for me to take care of myself.

It was time to sober up from boyhood whimsy.

It was time for me to get real courage.

It was time for me to become a man.

Although the production team told me to take all the time away I needed, my family insisted I go back to Austin and finish the job I'd started. Four days after the wake I drove back and was on the set that night.

We were shooting one of the final scenes of the film on the football field that evening. Again, I had no lines in the scene but Linklater wanted me in it. Walking around the stadium at sunset before the night's filming started, Rick and I were talking about life, loss, and *what it's all about.*

"I think it's about livin, man," I said. "Even though my dad's no longer physically here, his spirit is still alive in me for as long as I keep it alive. I can still talk to him, do my best to live by what he taught me, and keep him alive forever."

I immortalized this idea that very night in a scene where Randall "Pink" Floyd is deciding whether or not to sign the "no drug" pledge to stay on the football team.

August 2, 1992 *

"You gotta do what Randall 'Pink' Floyd wants to do, man,

and lemme tell you this, the older you do get,

the more rules they're gonna try-yyyy to get you to follow,

you just gotta just keep livin, man, l-i-v-i-n."

just keep livin . . . lower case because life is nobody's proper noun, and there's no "g" on the end of livin because life's a verb.

j.k. livin

The three weeks I played Wooderson in *Dazed and Confused* were difficult because of my loss, but graceful because of my gain. The prior year my dad had given me approval to do what I wanted to do but was never able to *see* me do it, but he *was* alive to see me start what I would finish, a hobby that became a career. I felt a certain serendipity in the fact that the end of my dad's life had overlapped with a new beginning in mine, on-screen, and off.

The three weeks of practical experience on the set of *Dazed and Confused* made me a much more competent director when I returned

* The last picture ever taken of my dad. He's in Navarre Beach, Florida, at the spot he dreamed of building his oyster shack if and when he ever "hit a lick" and retired.

to film school as a senior that fall. I directed a documentary about the Hispanic lowrider culture in the South called *Chicano Chariots* that I was proud of. The same year, I acted in what I could, starring in an *Unsolved Mysteries* episode and another music video. I was ready to graduate and take "I would if I could" to "I can and I am."

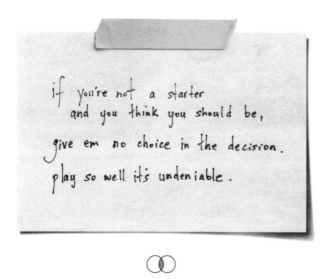

if you're not a starter
and you think you should be,
give em no choice in the decision.
play so well it's undeniable.

My plan was to drive out to Hollywood the day after graduation and sleep on Don Phillips's couch until I could get paying work as an actor or in film production. The production manager on *Dazed*, Alma Kuttruff, had me penciled in to work as a production assistant on the set of the next Coen Brothers film, *The Hudsucker Proxy*, which was scheduled to commence filming in a few months.

But first, I booked a one-day gig in a local Austin film production, *Texas Chainsaw Massacre: The Next Generation*. The role was that of a "Romeo to Renée Zellweger's Juliet," a motorcycle man in black leather and shades who mysteriously rides past her school at the beginning of the film, then returns at the end, after she's survived a night from hell, to pick her up and ride off into the sunset. I don't think I had any lines.

A couple of days before the Saturday shoot I met with the director, Kim Henkel, who asked if I knew any male actors who might be right for the lead role of Vilmer, the killer with a mechanical leg who drives a tow truck. I gave him the names of two actors I knew from the Donna Adams Talent Agency.

With a U-Haul already packed to the ceiling and hitched to the back of the four-cylinder Dodge pickup truck I'd named "Surf Longview," I swung by the small home that was the production office to pick up the two scenes I'd be shooting that weekend. Come Monday it would be time to *head west young man* and chase down my Hollywood dreams.

With the two scenes in hand, I exited the house and walked up the small asphalt footpath that led through the unmowed St. Augustine yard to the curb where I'd parked. As I unlocked my driver's-side door, opened it, and began to step into the cab, a thought occurred to me. *Why don't I try out for the role of Vilmer?*

I stepped out of the opened door, shut it behind me, and strode back down the walkway to the office door and without knocking, went inside.

"Hey, Matthew, you forget something?" Kim asked.

"Yeah, I did. I wanna try out for that role of Vilmer."

Clearly surprised, Kim said, "Well, sure, that's a great idea, when do you wanna try it?"

"Right now," I said without thinking.

"Well, we don't have any actresses here, it's just you, me, and Michelle," he said. I looked at Michelle, the secretary behind her desk.

"I'll do it," she said.

"You mind if I try and scare the shit out of you?" I asked.

"No, that's fine, go for it," she gamely said.

I went to the kitchen and grabbed an oversized metal kitchen spoon, stalked back into the room *as* Vilmer, and with a mechanical leg limp I skidded Michelle's desk out of my way, pinned her in the corner, and proceeded to make her cry in fear.

"You got the part if you want it," Kim said.

"Yeah, that was great, it was *really* scary," Michelle agreed.

I'd taken a chance and I'd gotten the part. Shooting would last four weeks.

With all I owned already packed in the U-Haul and a terminated lease on the apartment I'd been livin in, I called a buddy who had a spare couch. My trip west was going to have to wait another month because I had my second role in a movie. I was going to play Vilmer, a tow-truck-driving killer with a mechanical leg and a missing remote to control it.

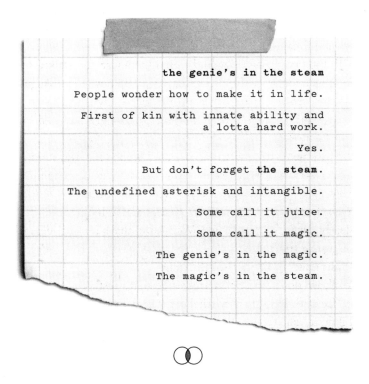

```
            the genie's in the steam
    People wonder how to make it in life.
    First of kin with innate ability and
                    a lotta hard work.
                                    Yes.
            But don't forget the steam.
    The undefined asterisk and intangible.
                Some call it juice.
                Some call it magic.
            The genie's in the magic.
            The magic's in the steam.
```

Four weeks and four thousand bucks later, Surf Longview, a loaded U-Haul, and I hit the I-10 freeway for the twenty-four-hour drive to Hollywood.

My adrenaline pumping for arrival, I'd been driving for just over twenty hours straight when I got to Indio, California. That's when I saw a sign for an exit that read SUNSET DR. Drive? Lane? Boulevard? *Who cares, that has to be the exit for the one and only legendary* Sunset Boulevard. It was 8 P.M.

Damn, I'm making good time, I thought as I hit the gas.

Back in Austin, I'd made plans to play the CD that was now perched on my passenger seat, the Doors' *L.A. Woman*, upon my inaugural entrance into Hollywood. I put it in and cranked up the volume, Ray Manzarek's keyboard and Jerry Scheff's bass line began setting my stage. I turned it up louder, the soundtrack of my one and only introduction to Hollywood, California, pumping through my speakers and veins.

Well, Sunset Drive is *not* Sunset Boulevard. As a matter of fact, Sunset Drive off the I-10 West is about 162 miles from Sunset Boulevard off the same freeway. Not knowing this at the time, I listened to the song "L.A. Woman" twenty-two times in a row thinking the lights of Hollywood were just over the next hill.

At 10:36 P.M., I arrived at Don Phillips's house on the beach in Malibu. I rang the bell. Nothing. I rang it again.

"Yeah, yeah, yeah, who is it?!" Don finally said from the other side of the door.

"It's me, McConaughey!" I yelled.

"Oh yeah, McConaughey, ya think you can come back later? I got this little chippy in the back."

Exhausted from the twenty-four-hour drive and the overexertion from the premature anticipation of Sunset Boulevard, I barked, "Fuck, no, I can't come back later, I told you I'd be getting here tonight. I just drove from Austin!"

Don opened the door, buck naked with a boner.

"Yeah, you're right," he said. "Gimme twenty minutes." Then he shut the door on me.

Welcome to Hollywood.

GREENLIGHT.

Life was good at Don's and the couch was comfortable. Every night he cooked us a filet mignon, followed up with one scoop of vanilla Häagen-Dazs ice cream topped with strawberry marmalade that he always announced, in his best French accent, as the "pi-*ece* de re-*sistance*!" And there was always a fresh bottle of Stolichnaya chilling in the freezer. Still, I needed a job.

I was notified that production on *The Hudsucker Proxy* had been moved to an unidentified date later in the year, so that PA job I was relying on was no more. I was getting anxious, ready to go to work, land an agent, read a script, audition for something, or if I had to, get another PA job. Neither was happening and Don was the only guy I knew in town.

One night over a tenderloin I casually said, "Hey, Don, you think you can get me a meeting with an agent, man? I only got a few grand to my name and I *need* to get some work."

HOLLYWOOD.

Want her don't need her.

Do this and you have a chance, don't, you won't.

Forever for rent, never to own, the one we all lust for, the constant unknown.

The unattainable white buffalo that dares divinity with every moonlit tryst.

Does she even exist?

The answer's what we need, the question's what we want.

Want her don't need her,

and she might give it up.

Don snapped. "You shut that fuckin talk up right now! This town smells *needy;* you are done for before you even get started, you hear me!!! You *need* to be cool. You *need* to get the fuck outta here! Get out of town, go to Europe, anywhere! And don't come back until you're ready to not *need* it! Then we'll talk about an agency meeting, you hear me!"

He meant it, I knew he meant it, and I knew what he meant. He didn't have to tell me twice.

Cole Hauser, Rory Cochrane, and I had become friends on *Dazed and Confused,* and with some of my newly legislated spare time, we got together and decided we'd go to Europe for a month, rent motorcycles, and ride. We rounded up our backpacks and some petty cash, bought round-trip tickets to and from Amsterdam, then headed overseas.

After landing, we rented a car and headed south, where we found a first-class motorcycle shop in Rosenheim, Germany. Wearing sleeveless shirts and dirty jeans we shared our plans to bike across Europe with the shop's owner, Johan.

"Let's find you the best motorcycles for your adventure," he said.

Cole chose a big bull of a bike, a Kawasaki 1000. Rory, a Ducati Monster M900. Me, a BMW 450 Enduro,* All brand-new, never-ridden-before bikes. Perfect. Johan tallied the bill, over $12,000.

"We don't have the money to rent these for a month," I said.

"Well, how much *do* you have?" he asked.

"Enough to rent em for three days," Rory answered.

Johan took a deep breath and a long look at us. His hairy-armpitted wife stood in the background, not happy with his breath *or* his look.

"When I was a young man your age, I toured Europe on a motorbike with my friends. I opened this shop so people like you could

---

* Turns out an Enduro 450 is not the way to ride through Europe on the autobahn. If your motorcycle does only 105 mph, you're gonna get blown off the road by the eighteen-wheelers and V12 sedans cruise controlling at 180.

explore the same way I did. You *need* to take these bikes. You need to *ride* these bikes," Johan said with certainty.

"But we don't have enough money, all we can offer you is $400 apiece."

"Do not trust them," his hairy-armpitted wife said. "They may never bring them back if you do."

"Yes, we will, you can have our economy-class airline tickets back to America as security if you need it," I said.

His wife knew where this transaction was heading and didn't like it. She violently shook her head no.

"Four hundred apiece is twelve hundred total, pay me that and you go have fun for a month on these motorbikes," he said. "I don't want your return tickets for insurance. Go, ride, explore, have an adventure, and I want to hear the stories when you return."

We couldn't believe our luck. We smiled at each other as Johan gave each of us a friendly bear hug, saying, "Have fu-*uuunnn*." We began to roll our brand-new motorcycles from the showroom floor.

"Not so fast," the hairpit interrupted. "I'll take those plane tickets."

We handed them over, then rode out of that parking lot, leaving a proud and serene Johan in the rearview mirror, his wife scolding obscenities in his ear as he watched us ride away.

We crossed Germany, Austria, the Swiss Alps, Italy. It was a geographic splendor, and what a way to see it. About eleven days into our ride, we were approaching the seaside town of Sestri Levante, Italy, when Rory laid the Ducati down doing 120 getting off the autobahn exit. Somehow, he came out of it with only minor cuts, bruises, a night in the hospital, and some mangled leather pants. But the brand-new Ducati Monster M900 was totaled.

Rory called Johan the next day with the bad news. "I wrecked the Ducati, Johan. I totaled the bike."

"Wait, Rory, you wrecked?" Johan asked. "Are you okay?"

"Yeah, I'm okay, but the bike, it's totaled. I'm sorry, man."

"I don't care about the bike as long as you're okay."

121

"I'm fine," Rory replied.

"Good, where is the bike?"

"It's in a field just off exit 74 into Sestri Levante."

"Okay, I'll send a truck and driver to you now. He should be there by tomorrow afternoon to pick up the totaled bike. Meet him there. I'm happy you are okay."

The next day around 3:00 P.M., the three of us were waiting in the field next to the mangled Monster when a large cargo truck showed up. Johan was behind the wheel. He greeted us warmly, eyed the totaled Ducati, then opened the back of the truck.

As Rory, Cole, and I moved to load the wrecked cycle into the truck, Johan unloaded something else from it. *Another* brand-new Ducati Monster M900. "I am glad you are okay," he said. "Keep riding."

So we did.

Thousands of miles and three weeks later we returned to Johan's shop in Rosenheim on our bikes, no longer brand-new, but none of them totaled.

Johan greeted us in the parking lot with bear hugs on arrival.

"Come inside for a coffee and tell me all about your adventures," he said with a smile.

"It was epic," I said. "We raced the autobahns, drank from the Austrian rivers, traversed the Swiss Alps, had dinners in Mussolini's hideout, and raved in Rimini till sunrise."

"Thank you, Johan, it was the best trip we've ever taken," Cole said.

After a couple hours of tale telling, our rental car was delivered and it was time to head back to Amsterdam so we could fly home the next day. Johan's wife grudgingly handed us back our plane tickets home.

Johan in Rosenheim. What a mensch.

I hadn't thought about getting an agent or a job the entire month. I headed back to Malibu with lifelong friends and more great stories to tell.

GREENLIGHT.

dirt roads and autobahns

The road less traveled may not be a dirt
road; for some, it may be the autobahn.

Robert Frost was right, taking the road
less traveled can make all the difference.

But that road isn't necessarily the road
with the least traffic.

It may be the road that we, personally,
have traveled less.

The introvert may need to get out of the
house, engage with the world, get public.

The extrovert may need to stay home and
read a book.

Sometimes we need to get *out* there,
sometimes we need to get *in* there.

Some days our road less traveled is a
solitary dirt trail.

On others it's the subway on the 7 line.

THE ART
OF RUNNING
DOWNHILL

DON LOVED THAT I HAD gone on the motorcycle trip through Europe with "his boys!" The three of us, all cast by *him* in *Dazed and Confused*. Back sleeping on his couch, I didn't say a word about meeting an agent. Didn't even think about it. Didn't *need* to.

One night, over another scoop of vanilla Häagen-Dazs and some strawberry marmalade, Don said, "You're ready. Tomorrow morning, I got us a meeting with Brian Swardstrom and Beth Holden at the only agency that would see us, the William Morris Talent Agency. Tell em you wanna direct as well, you'll sound even *less* needy, they'll salivate."

My résumé was my performance as Wooderson in *Dazed and Confused*, which had been released in limited theaters a few months earlier. (*Texas Chainsaw Massacre: The Next Generation* hadn't been released yet.)

Boots, jeans, and a tucked-in button-down, I shook their hands and sat down for my next job interview. I acted like I wanted them, not like I needed them. Swardstrom nibbled, Holden bit. I signed with Beth and William Morris the next day.

Now, this is usually the point in the story where the protagonist, the young wannabe actor gone west, grovels and lines up hundreds of "almost got it" auditions, has to take a job waiting tables, and gets asked to suck somebody's dick for a cameo role.

Well, that's not my story.

One week after signing with William Morris, I got my first audition in Hollywood with casting director Hank McCann for the role of Drew Barrymore's very honest husband "Abe Lincoln" in the film *Boys on the Side*. They liked my audition enough to schedule a second one for director Herb Ross six weeks later. A week after *that* first audition I got called in for another one, this time for a Disney film called *Angels in the Outfield*. The role was that of an "all-American baseball player named Ben Williams." I wore my American flag baseball cap and a white T-shirt for *this* job interview. Warner Bros. lot, Bungalow 22, parking-lot level. I opened the door to enter, backlit by the afternoon sun.

"Whoa! Look at you! All-American kid!" a voice boomed from a couch opposite the entry door.

I stopped in the doorway and looked down at the squinting man who was addressing me. "Yes, sir," I said.

"You ever play baseball?" he asked.

"Twelve years, from six years old till I was eighteen."

"Great, you got the job, we start shooting in two weeks!"

$48,500 to play baseball for ten weeks in Oakland. *You kiddin me?* And I needed it, I only had $1,200 to my name at the time.

I called my brother Pat to share the news.

"Fuck, yeah, little brother. Super Bowl's comin up, let's go to Vegas and celebrate. On me!"

GREENLIGHT.

128

Now, I like to gamble. Mostly on myself but occasionally on sports, specifically NFL football. I never bet enough to change my lifestyle, win or lose, but rather, just enough to *buy a ticket to the game,* meaning, enough to make me want to watch it closely and give a damn, enough to get a *buzz.* For me, that can be $50. I've never used a tout service (expert "pickers") because to me, what's the fun in that? If I lose, I try to figure out where I misread the matchup, but ultimately I like to pick my own winners because when I win, I *kn-ewww* it.

When I win, it was so easy, such a clear choice, a lead-pipe cinch. I'm a fortune-teller, Nostradamus, a magician, all because I fucking *kn-ewww* it. That's what I love about betting, and I give a lot more credit to the *I kn-ewww it*s than I do to the *What the fuck happened?*s. I bet for the entertainment value, the enjoyment I get when I *kn-ewww* it.

When betting, I specifically enjoy considering the intangibles. The *bet on San Francisco at home to cover against Baltimore because Baltimore will be jet-lagged from the long flight West* bet. The *take Brett Favre and the Packers on Monday night because his dad passed away last Tuesday* or *bet on any team who has a star player who just had his first newborn child because they're now playing for more than themselves* bet. The *bet against the Philadelphia Eagles because they're playing their first game in their new stadium and have Sylvester Stallone, aka Rocky Balboa, there to commemorate it, because it's too much celebration about stuff OFF the football field* bet. When I win these bets based on these psychological hunches and tells that are neither scientific nor measured by the Vegas line makers, I believe I have an inside track, betting 5.0, Machiavellian craft, all because I *kn-ewwww* it.

I flew Southwest Airlines to Vegas for the big game, the second year in a row the Dallas Cowboys and the Buffalo Bills would meet in the

129

Super Bowl. An agent, a 48,500-dollar job in hand, a weekend of black-jack, boozing, and football with my brother Pat. I was flying high.

The Dallas Cowboys were a powerhouse that season: Troy Aikman, Emmitt Smith, Charles Haley, Michael Irvin. They had drubbed the Bills in the previous Super Bowl and opened as 10.5-point favorites in this one. The line was stretching further in Dallas's favor, already up to 12.5.

The Saturday night before Super Bowl Sunday Pat and I dominated the blackjack table for eleven straight hours and walked out of the casino at daybreak up big. I'd won almost two thousand bucks and Pat was up over four grand—major money for both of us at the time.

We woke up Sunday around noon and started strategizing on who we were going to bet on and why.

"I think +10.5 was too many points to begin with and it's already up to +13 at the Aladdin," I said. "Second time's a charm, let's go Bills."

"Shi-iit, I think they might even upset the Cowboys money line (straight-up win)," Pat said. "Let's round the wagons with the Bills and hammer em every which way."

An hour before kickoff, we found a casino that had Buffalo at an astronomically high +14.5 and placed our bets. We put our money together, six grand total, and laid our bets on the Bills in every way you can imagine.

4g to cover the 14.5 point spread.
1g to win 3.2g on Bills money line.
$250 at 8 to 1 that Thurman Thomas gets more yards than Emmitt Smith.
$250 at 12 to 1 that Andre Reed has more yards than Michael Irvin.
$250 at 6 to 1 that Jim Kelly throws for more yards than Troy Aikman.
$100 at 18 to 1 that Bruce Smith is the MVP.
$100 at 4 to 1 that Dallas has more than 1.5 turnovers.

We bet every penny we had except $100 for our beer.

At halftime the Bills were up 13–6. We were dancing, singing, and buying doubles. "Holy shit, we're gonna upgrade to first class for the flight home. We're geniuses. And we were getting 14.5 points! We *kn-ewww* it.

But you know what happened, right? Dallas scored 24 unanswered points in the second half and not only won the game, but covered the 14.5 point spread 31–13.

Emmitt Smith outrushed Thurman Thomas.

Michael Irvin had more yards than Andre Reed.

Jim Kelly did not have more passing yards than Troy Aikman.

Bruce Smith was not the MVP, and Dallas turned the ball
over only once.

We lost every single bet we placed. Every. One.

Heads hanging, our buzz turning into fatigue, we walked out of the casino and hailed a cab to take us back to the hotel with twenty bucks between us. A dusty yellow '86 Bonneville with its back-left bumper grazing the pavement pulled up. "Holiday Inn," we said as we got in.

Behind the wheel was a shaggy old guy who hadn't shaved in three months or showered in three days. Clearly taking interest in our defeated body language, he reached up to his rearview mirror and tilted it to get a better look at us as he pulled away from the curb.

Pat and I were staring out our backseat windows in stunned silence, wondering what the hell had just happened, when an all-knowing voice boomed through the cab, "Bet on the Bills, did ya!? Coulda told ya that was a stupid-ass bet. I *kn-ewww* the Cowboys were gonna kill em, ya fuckin losers!"

Pat stared ice picks into the guy through the rearview mirror, then, exploded.

"Oh, yeah, motherfucker!? If you *kn-ewww* the Cowboys were gonna cover, then what the FUCK are you doing driving a cab!"

Everybody likes to be in the know. Even when we lose two and win one, we believe *the one* more than the two. We believe *the one* winner we picked was a product of our truer selves, was when we met our potential and read the future, was when we were gods. The two losses, however, were aberrations, misfits, glitches in our masterminds, even though the math clearly makes them the majority. After the game is played, everybody *kn-ewww* who the winner would be. Everybody is lying. Nobody *kn-owwws* who's going to win or cover the bet, there is no *sure thing*, that's why it's called *a bet.* There's a reason Vegas and Reno continue to grow. They *kn-owww* we bettors love to believe we do. That *is* a lock.

MOST OF THE TIME IT'S NOT STOLEN, IT'S RIGHT WHERE YOU LEFT IT.

A month into shooting *Angels in the Outfield,* the studio behind *Boys on the Side* flew me back to Hollywood for my follow-up audition in front of director Herbert Ross. I'd been rehearsing for the part every night after playing baseball and was confident I had a take on *my man.* Herbert liked my audition and I got offered the role.

My very first audition in Hollywood had gotten me a second audition that landed me the fourth lead in a major motion picture drama starring Drew Barrymore, Mary-Louise Parker, and Whoopi Goldberg. It also got me a major paycheck of 150 grand.

As soon as I finished playing baseball in Oakland, I headed to Tucson, Arizona, where we'd be shooting *Boys on the Side.* Instead of the hotel where most others were staying, I rented a quaint adobe guesthouse on the edge of the Saguaro National Park outside of town. I rescued a black Lab–chow mix puppy from the local pound and named her Ms. Hud, after Paul Newman's character in one of my favorite films. The house came with a maid. I'd never had a maid before.

One Friday night after work, a friend of mine, Beth, came over for dinner and drinks. Like a kid on Christmas morning, I was telling her all the things I was so happy about in my new digs—the mud-brick architecture, the national park as my backyard, the fact that it came with a maid. Especially the maid.

"She cleans the place *after* I go to work, *washes* my clothes, *does* the dishes, puts fresh water *by my bed,* leaves me *cooked* meals—and, *she even presses my jeans*!" I told Beth, holding up my Levi's to show her the crisp, starched-white line running down the legs. Beth smiled at my enthusiasm, then said something I hadn't ever thought to ask myself, and haven't forgotten to since.

"That's great, Matthew, *if you want your jeans pressed.*"

I'd never had my jeans pressed before.

I'd never had anyone to press my jeans before.

I'd never thought to ask myself *if* I wanted my jeans pressed before because for the first time in my life I *could* have them pressed.

The never-before-offered opulent option now being a reality, *of course* I wanted my jeans pressed.

Or did I?

No, actually. I didn't.

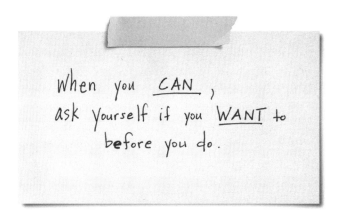

When you _CAN_,
ask yourself if you _WANT_ to
before you do.

After *Boys on the Side,* I returned to Malibu, now with my own loft on the beach. I started taking acting classes for the first time because I thought it was time to start *learning* the craft that I had practically fallen into. In the past, I'd always just gone with my instincts and they had served me well. Now, I was back in school, getting an education on *how* to read a script, *what* to look for, how to *prepare* for a role, how to *study.* How to be, I thought, a *professional* actor.

Meanwhile, I hadn't gotten work in the six months since wrapping *Boys on the Side.* I hadn't worked since I started taking those acting classes. I'd had a lot of auditions, and quite a few callbacks, but I couldn't seem to land a gig. I wondered why. I noticed I was more uptight and not taking as many risks in the auditions as I used to. I was tense. I was earnest. I was literal. I was heady. The new intellectual exercise had me getting in my own way.

the INTELLECT

Is not meant to surpass the apparent so far as to conceal it or make it *more* confusing.

It is meant to expose the truth *more* clearly and reveal *more* of the obvious from *more lines of sight.*

It should simplify things, not make them *more* cerebral.

Finally, I received a blind offer for a minor role in a small independent film called *Scorpion Spring*. I'd only be in one scene. They offered ten grand and I took it. No audition, shooting in two weeks. That's all I knew.

I decided that was all I *wanted* to know. I got the script and I didn't read one page of it, not a word, not even of the scene I was in. Why? Because I had a bright idea.

To lubricate my creative juices and rid myself of all the theoretical tension I'd been carrying since that last movie and those classes, I decided I was going to *go back* to how I acted when I first started, when I played this guy named David Wooderson, when reading just one line of the script completely unlocked the character for me.

It was easy for me to improvise in all those other unscripted scenes in *Dazed and Confused* because I was confident I knew who my man was, comfortable to just *say and do* what Wooderson would in any scene the director put me in. Back when I was all instinct, a natural.

Well, that's what I've been missing, I said to myself. *Enough of this academic, tight-minded, learn-ed studying shit I've been doing, it's time to return to my roots.*

In *Scorpion Spring, my man* was an "American drug runner in South Texas who meets up with the Mexican coyotes smuggling his dope back into the States," who then "reneges on the deal, doesn't pay for the smuggled drugs, and instead, kills the smugglers and takes the cocaine for free."

That's all I needed to know. Just *be* that guy, *handle* the situation like *he* would, improvise, do what *my man* would do. Easy.

Two weeks later, I'm on location in my trailer.

I know my man. I've created my backstory of an upper-midlevel drug runner who works for the cartel on the American side in Texas. I need the cocaine *and* the money and I'm carrying a loaded pistol, willing to kill to get out alive with both. I even look the part: unshaven, greasy hair, black boots, leather jacket. Who needs a script? I know who I am. Press record. I got this.

Time to go to set. Time to shoot the scene. No problem.

I arrive in character. I don't talk to anyone. I don't introduce myself to the other actors in the scene with me because *my man doesn't care about them and my man is going to kill them in this scene anyway. I just want my cocaine for free.*

Just before we take our marks a production assistant comes up to me, "Some sides,* Mr. McConaughey?" I take them and just shove them in my pocket without looking at them. All the actors settle onto their marks and prepare for "action." Here we go.

Well, I guess I lost my nerve a little bit because I decide it would be a good idea, right at *this* moment, *just* before we roll the camera, to have a quick peek at the scene and the dialogue. My thinking at the time? *If it's written well, I'll immediately remember the written lines because obviously that's what my man would say, and if it's not written well, then, I'll just be my man and do and say what he would do and say anyway.*

I unfold the sides and have a look.

One page.

Two pages.

Three pages.

Four pages . . .

Of a monologue . . .

In Spanish.

Holy shit. I feel a bead of sweat form on the back of my neck. My heart starts racing. *What am I going to do?* My mouth goes dry. I try to keep calm. And then I look up to no one in particular and aloud to the set, I say, "Can I get twelve minutes, please?"

My half-ass thinking was that twelve minutes would be: (1) enough time to memorize all the Spanish because, *Hey, I took a semester of*

---

* Sides are a miniature version of the scripted scene for the day.

Spanish class in the eleventh grade, and (2) not enough time to inconvenience the crew.

I take a little walk with the sides. A twelve-minute walk to be precise. I then return to set, put the sides back in my pocket, and step to my mark. The director says "action" and we shoot the scene.

I have never watched *Scorpion Spring.*

I did learn a good lesson that day, though.

We have to **prepare** to have freedom.

We have to do the **work** to then do the job.

We have to prepare for the job so we can be **free** to do the work.

Knowing my man does not mean I know Spanish.

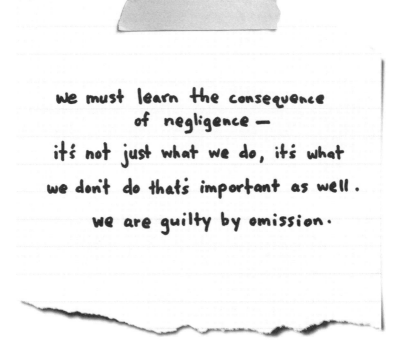

we must learn the consequence
of negligence —
it's not just what we do, it's what
we don't do that's important as well.
we are guilty by omission.

A few months later, having quit the acting classes but learned my lesson, I was back on the Warner Bros. lot in director Joel Schumacher's office to discuss a possible role in his next film, *A Time to Kill,* based on the book by John Grisham.

The irresponsibility of my half-cocked idea not to fully prepare for that last part had value. I was embarrassed, the embarrassment pissed me off, and that rage made me more daring.

Joel and I were meeting to discuss the part of "Freddie Lee Cobb," a young head of the Ku Klux Klan in a small Mississippi town. I *had* read the script this time, I'd even read the book. "Freddie Lee Cobb" was a strong and stirring role, but it wasn't the one I wanted. No, the *man* I wanted was the lead, "Jake Brigance," a young lawyer who defends a black man for killing the men who raped his daughter. I showed up in Joel's office that day with a plan.

Wearing a sleeveless John Mellencamp T-shirt and casually smoking a Marlboro, I sat across the desk from him.

"I think you'd be a great Freddie Lee Cobb, Matthew," he said.

"Yeah, I do, too, Mr. Schumacher. I understand where he came from and why he is who he is but . . . Who's playing the lead role of Jake Brigance?"

Joel paused and cocked his head a bit. "I don't know," he said. "Who do *you* think should?"

I leaned back in my chair, took a healthy drag, and on the exhale, looking him dead in the eyes, said, "I think *I* should."

Joel burst into laughter. "Ahhhh! I think that's a *great* idea, Matthew, but it is *never* going to happen! The studio will *never* put a relatively unknown actor in the lead role."

I stubbed out my cigarette and held his gaze.

I had pulled off the first part of my plan.

if only

Means you wanted something but did not get it.

For some reason, either by your own incompetence or the world's intervention, it did not happen.

Sometimes this is just the breaks and we need to bow out gracefully.

But more often than we care to admit, we don't get what we want

because we quit early or we didn't take the necessary risk to get it.

The more boots we put in the back side of our *if onlys*, the more we will get what we want.

Don't walk the *it's too late it's too soon* tightrope until you die.

What happened next was certainly not part of my plan, but a lot of things that were out of my control went my way.

Sandra Bullock, who was already cast as "Ellen Roark" in *A Time to Kill,* had recently starred in a film called *While You Were Sleeping,* which had recently opened with a respectable first weekend of just under $10 million. But since I'd planted the seed with Joel, *While You Were Sleeping* had crept up to over $80 million in domestic box office revenue. It was a big hit and had made Sandra Hollywood's newest "greenlight" movie star, which meant that studios believed she was popular enough to headline a film. With an actress who could now open a film already cast in the number three supporting role in *A Time to Kill*, Warner Bros. was suddenly free to consider a less bankable actor for the lead role.

But did that mean Joel Schumacher started to take my suggestion seriously? Apparently not. They were considering my now great friend and brother from another mother, Woody Harrelson, for the role of Jake Brigance.

Then the plot twisted once again. Turns out author John Grisham also had casting approval on the role of Jake Brigance, as the character was based on himself. Also turns out that on March 7, 1995, a man named Bill Savage was murdered in Mississippi. The murderers, a young man and woman, said they were inspired by Mickey and Mallory, the characters brought to life by Woody Harrelson and Juliette Lewis in Oliver Stone's *Natural Born Killers*. Bill Savage was John Grisham's friend, and there was *no way* the guy who played Mickey in *that* film was going to play Jake Brigance in *this* one.

Filming was scheduled to commence in six to eight weeks in Canton, Mississippi. All the roles were cast. Except for Jake Brigance.

A couple of weeks later, I was on the rooftop of a Mexican restaurant in L.A. having a 4:00 P.M. margarita with my manager, Beth Holden, when my phone rang.

"I want you to come in for a screen test," Joel Schumacher said over the phone. It had been two months since I'd planted the seed. "We'll do it next Sunday in a small private studio off Fairfax so no one will know, because, even if you do great, it's such a long shot that the studio will approve you, I don't want the perceived *failure* to be on your résumé around town. The scene I want you to test with will be Jake's final summation."

Sunday came. It was Mother's Day. I called mine at daybreak.

"Don't walk in there like you *want* the role, Matthew, walk in there like you *own* it!"

Just what I needed to hear.

"Thanks, Mom. Happy Mother's Day."

```
we are all made for every moment
                 we encounter.

whether the moment makes us or we
              make the moment.

whether we are helpless in it or
                 on top of it,

     the predator or the prey.

we are made for that moment.
```

A black car picked me up at 11:00 A.M. and drove me to the studio on Fairfax. There was a makeup artist, a costume designer, a director of photography, and a crew of around thirty people. Around 1:00 P.M. I walked onto the set, which was a courtroom with twelve actors, all sitting in a set-made jury box. I was nervous, but I was prepared. Everyone quieted down and took their places.

"Whenever you're ready, Matthew," Joel said.

I caught my breath and began to enact the final summation just as it was written in the script until I finished it with the now classic line, "Now, imagine she's white."

I was good, not great. I had remembered my lines, hit all the beats, taken my time, and told the story well. More than passable but nothing special.

"Great, Matthew," Joel said, "now throw away the script and say what *you'd* say."

Therein lies Joel Schumacher's genius. Be you. You are the character. I loved *that* note. What *I* would say and do. How do *I* feel about a young virgin girl being raped by three vile men? What did they kill in her that day?

What if it was *my* sister? What if it was *my* daughter? It was Mother's Day.

I tossed the script off the set and out of my mind. I began to slowly pace, my eyes began to burn, and with rage building, I painted the dreadful pictures in my mind, then said what I saw. Not yet a father myself, *but a father being the only thing I ever knew I wanted to be,* I imagined *my* daughter getting raped. I forgot testing. I forgot time. I said and did things a lawyer in a courtroom would never say or do. I cussed. I spit. I painted cringeworthy pictures of a child's lost innocence with bloody words that could have put me in jail alongside those I was condemning. I got sick to my stomach. I got violent. I broke a sweat.

I nailed it.

Two weeks later, working on the set of *Lone Star* in Eagle Pass, Texas, in the full-moon desert at midnight, I got a phone call. It was Joel Schumacher and John Grisham.

"You wanna be Jake Brigance?"

"You're damn right I do!"

I ran off into the night until I was about a mile away from anyone. Then, with tears in my eyes, I dropped to my knees, faced that full moon, extended my right hand up to it, and said,

"Thank you."

GREENLIGHT.

A Roof is a man-made thing

January 3, 1993. NFL playoffs. Houston Oilers vs.
Buffalo Bills. Oilers up 28-3 at halftime, 35-3 early
in the third. Frank Reich and the Bills come back to win
41-38 in overtime for one of the greatest comebacks in
NFL history. Yeah, the Bills won, but they didn't really
beat the Oilers. The Oilers lost that game, they beat
themselves.

Why? Because at halftime they put a ceiling, a roof, a
limit on their belief in themselves, aka the "prevent
defense." Maybe they started thinking about the next
opponent at halftime, played on their heels, lost their
mental edge the entire second half, and voilà, they
lost. In a mere two quarters, defensive coordinator Jim
Eddy went from being called defensive coordinator of the
year and "the man first in line to be a head coach next
year" to a man without a job in the NFL . . . or even
college football the next year.

You ever choked? You know what I mean, fumbled at the
goal line, stuck your foot in your mouth when you were
trying to ask that girl on a date, had a brain freeze on
the final exam you were totally prepared for, lipped out
a three-foot putt to win the golf tournament, or been
paralyzed by the feeling of "Oh my god life can't get
any better, do I really deserve this?"

I have.

What happens when we get that feeling? We clench up,
get short of breath, self-conscious. We have an out-of-
body experience where we observe ourselves in the third
person, no longer present, now *not* doing well what we
are there to do. We become voyeurs of our moment because
we let it become bigger than us, and in doing so, we
just became *less involved* in it and *more impressed* with
it.

Why does this happen?

It happens because when we mentally give a person,
place, or point in time more credit than ourselves, we
then create a fictitious ceiling, a restriction, over
the expectations we have of our own performance in that
moment. We get tense, we focus on the outcome instead
of the activity, and we miss the *doing* of the deed. We
either think the world depends on the result, or it's
too good to be true. But it doesn't, and it isn't, and
it's not our right to believe it does or is.

Don't create imaginary constraints. A leading role, a . blue ribbon, a winning score, a great idea, the love of our life, euphoric bliss, who are we to think we don't deserve these fortunes when they are in our grasp? Who are we to think we haven't earned them?

If we stay *in process*, within ourselves, in *the joy of the doing*, we will never choke at the finish line. Why? Because we aren't thinking of the finish line, we're not looking at the clock, we're not watching ourselves on the Jumbotron performing. We are performing in real time, where the approach *is* the destination, and there is no goal line because we are never finished.

When Bo Jackson scored, he ran over the goal line, through the end zone, and up the tunnel. The greatest snipers and marksmen in the world don't aim *at* the target, they aim on the other side of it. When we truly latch on to the fact that we are going to die at some point in time, we have more presence in this one.

Reach beyond your grasp, have immortal finish lines, and turn your red light green, because a roof is a man-made thing.

The day of the opening of *A Time to Kill,* I strolled to my favorite deli on the Third Street Promenade in Santa Monica, California, to get a tuna fish sandwich on toasted sourdough with extra pickles and ketchup on the side.

It was like any other stroll down that Promenade for me. Four hundred or so people milling about. Three hundred ninety-six made nothing of me. Four did. A few girls who thought I was cute and one dude who liked my shoes.

That night, *A Time to Kill* premiered in theaters across America and grossed fifteen million dollars in its opening weekend—a box office hit in 1996.

The following Monday I went back to the Promenade to get another tuna fish sandwich on toasted sourdough with extra pickles and ketchup on the side.

It was *not* like any other stroll down that Promenade for me. Four hundred or so people milling about. Three hundred ninety-six stared at me. Four did not. Three babies and a blind man.

I checked my fly and lightly thumbed my nose to see if I had a booger hanging out.

I didn't.

What the fu-*uuuuck?*

I was famous.

sometimes you have etc.

sometimes etc. has you.

-Fatima Alves

The hype surrounding my "arrival" was off the charts. Being hailed as *the next big thing*, "Matthew McConaughey Saves the Movies" was the boldface caption behind my head on the cover of certain industry magazines. *Save the movies?* Hell, I didn't *know* they needed saving, and if they did, I wasn't sure I was or wanted to be the one to save them.

I just wanted to act, to play roles that interested me in stories that mattered to me.

From that day on, the world became a mirror. Strangers laid their hands on me and spoke to me like they knew me well. Actually, they weren't strangers at all anymore.

People I'd never seen or met before would approach me and say, "My dog had cancer, too, I'm so sorry about Ms. Hud . . ."

How'd you know I had a dog? How'd you know her name? How'd you know she might have cancer? What happened to introducing yourself?

Everyone had a preconceived bio of me now.

Honest first impressions were a thing of the past. That check had been cashed.

My world had changed. In the words of James McMurtry, "Now it's upside down and backwards, the foot's on the other shoe."

Everyone *loved* me now, and they weren't shy to say it out loud and often.

Me, I'd only said it to four people in my life.

Anonymous no more and forever.

The same happened with scripts.

The Friday *before* opening weekend there were one hundred scripts I wanted to do. Ninety-nine nos. One yes. The Monday *after*?

Ninety-nine yeses. One no.

Wow.

Awesome.

Shit.

What was real? What was not? The sky just opened up to me and it was tough to feel the ground beneath my feet. My differential split, my spiritual foundation in flight, I needed some gravity. It was time to bend my knee bone.

Why we all need a walkabout

Noise-to-signal ratio.

We are more constantly
bombarded by unnatural
stimuli than ever before.

We need to put ourselves
in places of decreased
sensory input so we can
hear the background
signals of our
psychological processes.

As the noise decreases,
the signals become
clearer,

we can hear ourselves
again, and we reunite.

Time alone simplifies the
heart.

Memory catches up,
opinions form.

We meet truth again, and
it teaches us,

landing on stable feet
between our reaching out
and retreat, letting us
know we are not lonely in
our state, just alone.

Because our unconscious
mind *now* has room to
reveal itself, we see it
again.

It dreams, perceives, and
thinks in pictures, which
we *now* can observe.

In this solitude, we
then begin to *think* in
pictures, and actualize
what we see.

Our souls become anonymous
again,

and we realize we are
stuck with the one person
we can never be rid of:
ourselves.

The Socratic dialogue
can be ugly, painful,
lonesome, hard, guilt-
ridden, and a nightmare
vicious enough to need a
mouth guard not to gnaw
our fangs into nubs while
we sweat cold in feverish
panic.

We are forced to confront
ourselves.

And this is good.

We more than deserve this
suffrage, we've earned it.

An honest man's pillow is
his peace of mind,

and no matter who's in our
bed each night, we sleep
with ourselves.

We either forgive or get
sick and tired of it.

Herein lies the evolution.

With nowhere to run,
and forced to deal with
ourselves, our ugly
everyday suppressions
break out of the zoo and
monkey around,

where we find our self
in the ring with them,
deciding, *no more,* or *let
it slide.*

Whatever the verdict, we
grow.

It's us and us, our always
and only company.

We tend to ourselves, and
get in good graces once
again.

Then we return to
civilization, able to
better tend to our
tendencies.

Why? Because we took a
walkabout.

The Monastery of Christ in the Desert sits in miles of undisturbed desert, on the banks of the Chama River, in Abiquiu, New Mexico. The thirteen-and-a-half-mile dirt road from the highway that leads you there is usually washed out, so you can't bring a car. Thomas Merton loved it there. He said this monastery was a place where people can go to "re-adjust their perspectives." I read about it in a book and thought, *That's what I need at this time. A spiritual realignment.* I was all messed up in the head. Lost in the excess of my newfound fame and struggling with a nondeserving complex, my now roofless existence not only had me searching for my bearings, it was bearing down on me. How could a working-class kid from Uvalde, Texas, be deserving of all this opulence and accolade? I didn't know how to navigate the decadence of my success, much less believe it was mine to enjoy. I didn't know who to trust, including myself. In the book, the brothers said that, "If you can get to us, just ring the bell, we'll take you in."

A good friend and I drove from Hollywood to that dirt road, where he dropped me off, and I made the thirteen-and-a-half-mile march to the monastery. I arrived an hour after sundown and rang the bell. Dressed in cowl and tunic, a short man named Brother Andre greeted me, "Welcome, brother, all travelers have a place to stay here."

I washed up and went to the group dinner where Psalms were read aloud and talking was strictly prohibited. Later, Brother Andre ushered me to a small, simple room with a cot and a sleeping mat on the floor where I lay down for the night.

The next day, I said to Brother Andre, "I need to talk about some things going on in my life and mind, do you know who I could talk to?"

"Yes," he said, "Brother Christian would be a good man for you to talk to about such things."

I met Brother Christian and we went for a long walk in the desert. I unloaded my feelings of guilt, the low and lecherous places my mind had been traveling, the perverseness of my thoughts. "Since becoming famous," I professed, "I've tried to be a good man, to not lie and deceive myself, to be more pure of heart and mind, but I am full of lust, objectifying other people and myself. I do not feel a connection to my past nor see the path to my future, I'm lost. I don't *feel* myself."

I shared the demons of my mind for three and a half hours with Brother Christian. I took myself to the woodshed. He did not say a word. Not. One. He just patiently listened as we wandered side by side through the desert.

At hour four we found ourselves back at the chapel sitting on a bench just outside the entrance. Now weeping, I eventually came to the end of my confession. We sat in silence while I awaited Christian's judgment. Nothing. Finally, in the unrest of the stillness, I looked up. Brother Christian, who hadn't said one word to me this entire time, looked me in the eyes and in almost a whisper, said to me,

"Me, too."

Sometimes we don't need advice. Sometimes we just need to hear we're not the only one.

GREENLIGHT.

Brother Christian

both are true

I'm an optimist by nature, my eye is high,
I have hope, and the man I want to be sleeps
in the same bed with the man I am, in head,
heart, spirit, and body. I don't always
enjoy my company because of that son of a
bitch Jiminy Cricket, but I am rarely able
to knock him off my shoulder either. And for
good reason.

Even when I'm out of tune, off frequency,
having trouble feeling any traction or
viscosity between my being and my actions, or,
alternately, when I am so lost in the music
that I am unaware, my best self is always
there, and he will start the Socratic dialogue
sooner than I choose to hear him and long
after I want to, because he's insatiable.

I, of course, eventually do hear him,
then the challenge becomes, to listen.
Once I do, and stop pitting fate against
responsibility, truth against fiction,
sins against who I wish I was, selfishness
against selflessness, mortality against
eternity, I learn, and then begin just being
who I am, and doing what I do, for me-not
for anyone else and for everyone else at the
same time. For me and God, together. Then I
realize I am responsible for fate, fiction
is truthful, a sinner and saint I am, an
egotistical utilitarian as well. I'll be
mortal forever.

Now, each step at a time has the big picture
in mind, and I am the man I want to be,
Jiminy Cricket is a bluebird on my shoulder,
and Socrates has one voice.

I didn't mishandle my newfound fame as much as I just didn't really
have a handle on it. I was numb, occasionally dumb, and picked a few

battles that did not need picking. If I was thrown off balance for a bit, it was mainly because I gave a damn, and it mattered to me what it all meant, and didn't. Mostly I danced lightly between the raindrops. I enjoyed being able to finally put super unleaded gasoline in my truck, picking up the tab when I went out with my friends, getting the backstage passes, and working with so many talented people. I tried to remain a gentleman and accept the caviar, fine wines, and "I love you"s with grace, but a lot of it felt like the maid was still pressing my jeans after I asked her not to. I made sure to call my mom every Sunday.

Only it wasn't my mom I was calling anymore.

It wasn't my mom who was listening to me.

It wasn't my mom who was talking to her son.

It was a woman who was more enamored with my fame than I was.

This was never more evident than when I got a call at home from a friend one night.

"Dude, are you watchin this?"

"Watchin what?"

"Put it on Channel 7, *Hard Copy*!" my friend says.

I turn on the tube. Put it on Channel 7 and . . .

There's my mother, talking to the camera that is following her through our house on a guided tour.

"And this is the bed where he lost his virginity to Melissa, I think her name was, anyway, doesn't matter, she didn't last . . . And *this* is his bathroom, just a shower, no bathtub, and you *know* what I caught him doing in *there*! Ha-ha, but trust me, it's no big deal, I've seen it plenty of times."

Oh. Shit.

I call Mom.

"Mom, what did you do?"

"What?"

"*Hard Copy*."

"What *Hard Copy*?"

"Mom, I'm watchin it right now; *you* are, too, I can hear it in the background!"

"Oh, *that* . . ."

"Yeah, *that*!"

"I didn't think you'd find out."

"Mom. It's on national television. How would I not find out!"

Sadly, my relationship with my mom was strenuous for the next eight years.

"Loose lips sink ships," I kept telling her. She tried. It didn't matter, she couldn't help herself. She wanted a piece of my fame, and while I was still finding *my* balance with it, I wasn't self-assured enough to share it with anyone else, especially my own mother. The more she wanted a piece of my place, the more I locked her out. If Dad were alive he would have loved my success, but unlike Mom, he would have been in the front row, not trying to steal my show.

With Mom, as soon as I'd show up she was saying *come back soon,* so I started leaving early. I'd give her an inch and she'd take a mile, so when she didn't meet me halfway, I started walking twice as slow to make her wait twice as long. I quit sharing *any* of my life or experiences with her; I couldn't trust her. I didn't need another friend on my band-wagon, I needed my *mom,* and unfortunately she was on *another* type of extended vacation.

Years later, with my feet more firmly on the ground and my career established, I finally said fuck it, and loosened the reins on her. She was in her seventies and I figured I might as well let her have all the fun she wants to, and to this day she does. She loves the red carpet, doing interviews, and telling the world she "*knows where I got it from.*" Her.

She's got a point.

```
the art of running downhill
Don't trip yourself while running downhill.
That mountain you wanna climb?
It's just around the corner.
Don't invent drama.
It will come on its own.
```

It'd been four months since *A Time to Kill* had been released and I was in high demand. Warner Bros., who I had signed a three-picture deal with prior to doing *A Time to Kill,* was anxiously anticipating my next role. Dozens of offers came my way, I even started a production company to create material of my own. I was hungry to go to work, I just didn't know *what* I wanted to do. One of my strengths has always been that I can find an angle on anything, but now, with the ability *to* do almost anything, that strength was a weakness. Every project looked possible to me.

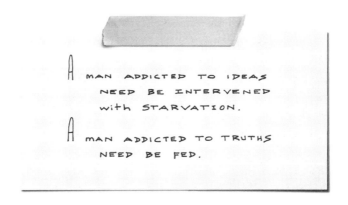

A MAN ADDICTED TO IDEAS
NEED BE INTERVENED
with STARVATION.

A MAN ADDICTED TO TRUTHS
NEED BE FED.

Feeling pressure to make a decision on my next movie, smothered by the blind affections of my recent fame, *and* having a new wildcard for a mom, I wanted to go somewhere where nobody knew my name. I needed to reaffirm that I, Matthew, not my *fame,* was justification for any adulation I received. I needed to go someplace where any affections I collected would be solely based on the man those strangers met and got to know *after* I arrived, not before. I needed to hear myself think— to check out to check in—so I could settle in to my new position of leverage and measure it, get less impressed with it, find some discernment, and figure out what kind of role, in what type of film, *I* wanted to do next. I needed some starvation. Then . . .

I HAD A WET DREAM.

Yes, the involuntary intercourse-, hands-, and fellatio-free nocturnal emission of semen one has while sleeping. Rare but welcomed, these lucid dreams most *common*ly involve a theme of sexual activity. This wet dream was not common.

I was seeing myself floating downstream on my back in the Amazon River, wrapped up by anacondas and pythons, surrounded by crocodiles, piranhas, and freshwater sharks. There were African tribesmen lined up shoulder to shoulder on the ridge to the left of me as far as my eyes could see.

I was at peace.

Eleven frames.

Eleven seconds.

Then I came.

I woke up.

Whoa.

All the elements of a nightmare but it was a wet dream.

GREENLIGHT.

What does it mean? I wondered.

There were two things I was sure about in the dream. One, I was on the *Amazon* River and two, those were *African* tribesmen on the ridge. I got out of bed and grabbed my World Atlas, then turned to the continent of Africa.

And started looking for the Amazon.

Well, as you probably know, you can look a mighty long time for the Amazon River in the continent of Africa because you're not going to find it. I looked for that river for two hours until I realized . . .

Wrong continent. The Amazon's in South America.

Damn, dreams can be tricky. Nevertheless, it was a sign, and just what I was looking for.

It was time to chase down my wet dream.

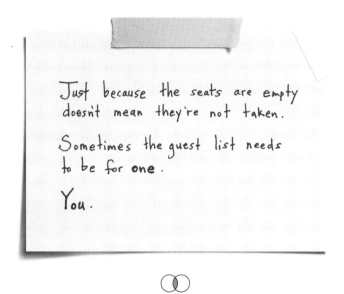

Just because the seats are empty doesn't mean they're not taken.

Sometimes the guest list needs to be for one.

You.

I crammed my backpack with minimal clothing, my journal, camera, medical kit, a hit of Ecstasy, and my favorite headband, then embarked on a twenty-two-day solo trip to Peru to find, and float, the Amazon River. Yes, the one in South America.

I flew to Lima, then on to Cuzco, where I met a guide and we mapped out my three-week journey to the Amazon River over *anti-cuchos** and pisco. I hiked the Andes and along the Urubamba River into the lost city of Machu Picchu listening to John Mellencamp's *Uh-Huh*† album on my Walkman as I climbed. Then, I took a bus, boat, and plane ride to get to the largest city in the world you can't get to by car, Iquitos, the "Peruvian capital of the Amazon."

---

* Grilled cow heart—the perfect first meal in a developing country. It'll get you sick early in the trip so you get sick less, later.

† *Uh-Huh* was an album my brother Pat turned me on to in 1983. My favorite tune on the album, "Pink Houses," has always been the most archetypal song about America for me—a song about generations, faith, and dreams lost and found, it was paramount in shaping the kind of patriot I was and am.

155

It was the twelfth night of my twenty-two-day adventure and I was settling into camp. I'd already hiked over eighty miles to this point and tomorrow I'd finally be in the waters of my wet dream, the Amazon River. Up to this point in the trip I'd had a hard time being present, so excited in anticipation of what the Amazon would mean to me, I had missed most of the beauties getting there. Still wrestling with my identity, I was guilt-ridden over sins of my past, lonely, and disgusted with the company I was keeping, my own.

In my tent, grappling with my demons, I couldn't sleep, so I quit trying to. Instead, I stripped off my clothes, along with every badge, banner, expectation, and affiliation I had on me. I discarded my American baseball cap that was my totem to patriotism, the Celtic knot pendant that symbolized my Irish heritage, the Lone Star flag amulet that stood for my Texas pride, and every other mascot of inspiration from adventures past. I even discarded the gold ring my father had given me that was made from a meltdown of his and my mom's class rings and gold from one of her teeth. I removed every idol that ever gave me comfort and security, pride, or confidence. All the window dressings and representations, the packaging around my product, was gone. I even punched myself in the face a couple of times for good measure. Who was I? Not only on *this* trip but in *this* life. Now naked and stripped down to nothing, I was only a *child of God,* and nothing more. Soaked in a cold sweat, I vomited until there was no bile left in my belly, then passed out from exhaustion.

Sometimes we have to leave what we know

to find out what we know

A few hours later, I awoke on the thirteenth morning to a rising sun. Surprisingly fresh and energized, I dressed, made some tea, and went for a morning walk. Not toward my destination or any expectation, but rather to nowhere in particular. I felt great—alive, clean, free, bright.

Walking along a muddy path, I turned a corner and there in the middle of the trail was a mirage of the most magnificent pinks and blues and red colors I had ever seen. It was electric, glowing, and vibrant, hovering just above the jungle floor, pulsing as if it was plugged in to some neon-charged power plant.

I stopped. I stared. I backed up a pace. There was no way around it and it was no mirage at all. The jungle floor in front of me was actually a kaleidoscope of thousands of butterflies. It was spectacular.

I stayed awhile gaping in wonder. Captivated, I heard this little voice inside my head say these words,

> *All I want is what I can see,*
> *all I can see is in front of me.*

No longer in a rush to get anywhere, or anticipating what was around the corner, coming up next, or up ahead, time slowed down. I raised my chin to the sky and said a quiet *thank you,* then glanced down the path just past the massive menagerie of levitating butterflies, and there, for the first time, I saw the Amazon River.

The tower of all my anxieties now lying down laterally in front of me just like that slow-moving river, for the first time in months I was at ease.

cont. - Yes, he plays a character, but the character is always
personal P.O.V and forms all opinions w/out personal bias. — I
of nature.. I am in the garden, and the freedom- song of pleasure
I dreamed of living here 1) for good 2) b/tween films 3) to write
They dance for a lady at daybreak & nightfall only. — I a
appreciate a place, a character, a time, I must think of i
goodness; God has such a colorful backyard ⊕ I believe th
he can see what he knows' — man must exit the comforts
the ears that listen, the pillows that he rests on — and fi
his mind has a thought, and his mouth goes to speak
and his God. In a time, in an America, when our lu
anywhere' with anyone, at anytime — by way of phone,
comforts of home, they are so hard to leave, and rightly
when we 'fear' leaving them, or not' having them b/c
jeopardy of losing our 'self' and our God. Technology
it is man-made, not God-given — So, man must exit civ
His may be, and watch, listen, see a place ● where no one
that has no choice' (mother Nature) so he can have no
survive, where he is, w/out luxuries, and survive where he
he needs, and we all know it is a necessary, to survive. I
truths and the soul, that and the freedom that has crosse
luxuries (phone, friends, t.v.,) are so clear and pure, that t
and mind. One must leave home if he is to find' home.
home. → Th. Just like we stop praying & seeking when we are
remember when there is unrest in our lives; man must le
to solve a problem. Act, don't react — and yes, the conflu
to leave
so go away from what you know, to find out what you know, a
is a luxury. Go away to your breeding ground, return, and
luxurious
[A smile I like has crossed my path, a walk I like has cro
[colors I see are brighter than before — I won't say I found
[opened the doors of my home and let them in. — I don'
want'. Everything I see is right in front of me. I want w
that I don't have here with me now.
Beliefs are better than conclusions b/c you can drive them
The Model T on the showroom floor, there for all to ooh and ahh

rom HIS P.O.V. whereas the chameleon disregards his
m understanding pleasure. Watch closely & listen to the ways
s all around me. Good night Mateo, I love you, dream sweetly
'be' 4) vacationing here. 4:45am. - up to watch Cock of Rocks
ld live here ½ the year realistically — I believe to
as a place to live permanently - find the likeness, the
t it is a necessity of man to leave what he knows so
the luxuries, the friendships, the advisors, the advice,
e himself "into a corner," into a place where, when
it, there is no one there to listen, but himself,
ries have b/come our necessities, when we can be
elevision, autos, planes, earphones, stereos ... oh, the
so, b/c I would not want to surrender mine, but
we 'fear' being able to survive, then we are in
basically 'good', but we must respect it as a luxury, b/c
'zation as we know it, go to the garden, wherever
n do anything for him but him 'self' — be in a place
ing but 'choice', he can do nothing but 'choose' how to
ll return, with the luxuries. Every man must know what
is hard to leave our place (home, U.S.A.) but the
my path, without the interruptions I welcome as
ey are places that are 'home' in every man's heart
Australia, Peru.) - Women with wet eyes make me feel d
eeling well (success, in the groove = luxuries) and only
ve his 'home' when, if not before it b/comes necessary
ty will come, as Gods reminder of our mortality,
d let necessity bear your luxuries, b/c necessity
do it with pleasure ; create, appreciate, respect. - I found
ed my path, a necklace I like, is around my neck,
hem, or own them now, b/c they found me, I simply
want to possess anything, there is nothing I really
t I see, and all I see, is in front of me : To be present
nstead of just look at them. Like Conclusions are
while belief is the 81 228 on the highway —
                    PRACTICALITY WINS OUT   11.8.96

A few hours later I returned to camp to pack for my continued journey. On arrival my guide called out to me in Spanish, "*Sois luz, Mateo, sois luz!*" Meaning, "You are light, Matthew, you are light!"

Now forgiven, I'd let go of the guilt, my confusion was gone, my penance felt paid. Back in good graces I shook hands with myself. From that morning on, I was present, embracing *only what I could see in front of me,* and giving it the justice it deserved. For the next two weeks I hiked, canoed, and even macheted my way through the Amazon rain forest on my one hit of Ecstasy.

And, yes, I *floated naked on my back down the Amazon River,* but no snakes, crocodiles, sharks, or piranhas enveloped me as they had in my dream. I guess they didn't have to anymore. On the final day, while bathing in the river, I did see what looked to be the final wave of a mermaid's tail as it slid beneath the water's surface heading downriver. I waved back.

I had crossed a truth. Did I find it? I don't know, I think it found me. Why? Because I put myself in a place to be found. I put myself in a place to receive it.

How do we know when we cross a truth or a truth crosses us?

I believe the truth is all around us all the time. The anonymous angels, the butterflies, the answers, are always right there, but we don't always identify, grasp, hear, see, or access them — because we're not in the right place to.

We have to make a plan.

GREENLIGHT.

God, when I
cross the
truth, give me

the **awareness**
to **receive** it

the
consciousness
to **recognize** it

the **presence** to
personalize it

the **patience** to
preserve it

and the **courage**
to **live** it

First, we have to **put
ourselves in the place** to
receive the truth. This
noisy world we live in,
with its commitments,
deadlines, fix thises, do
thats, and expectations
make it hard to get clarity
and peace of mind, famous
or not. So we have to
consciously put ourselves
in a place to receive that
clarity. Whether that's
prayer, meditation, a
walkabout, being in the
right company, a road
trip, whatever it is for
each of us.

Then, after we've put
ourselves in this place to
listen to the gospel and
hear their music, we then
have to be **aware enough to
receive** it, and **conscious
enough to recognize** it.
It will arrive nameless
because it is clear,
omnipresent, unanimous,
and infinite. It usually
lands like a butterfly,
quick and quiet. When we
let it in, it needs no
introduction.

Then the relationship can
begin, and we need the
presence to personalize
it. This is where the
anonymous truth gets
intimate, and becomes
autonomous. We ask our
self what it means, how
it's unique to us, and why
it's here now.

Then comes a harder part,
having the **patience to
preserve** it—getting
it from our intellect,
into our bones, soul,
and instinct. We must
pay attention to it,
concentrate on it, keep
it lit, and not let it
flutter away. This takes
commitment, time, and
'tendance.

If we make it *this* far,
after we've put ourselves
in the right place to
receive the truth,
recognized it as such,
made it our own, and
preserved it, then comes
the coup de grâce . . .

Having the **courage to live
it.** To actually walk away
from *that* place where it
found us, take that truth
with us into the screaming
arena of our daily lives,
practice it, and make it an
active part of who we are.

If we can do *that*, then we
are on our way to Heaven
on Earth.

**Where what we want is what
we need.**

**Where what we need is what
we want.**

I returned to Hollywood and soon made the decision to play the role of Palmer Joss opposite Jodie Foster in Robert Zemeckis's *Contact*. After my spiritual journey on the Amazon, my choice to inhabit a man who believed in God in a world of science was very close to the truth of where I was in my own life and where I wanted to spend my time in front of the camera. Jodie Foster was the clear lead and people questioned why I took "the girl's role," as they called it at the time, instead of taking other *leading* roles I was being offered. But I was more than satisfied with my choice, as I was interested in what I termed "philanthropic roles and stories of self-discovery," as well as working with great directors.

After we wrapped filming, I continued canoeing rivers, only now I was ready to row the highways of the United States, so I bought a 1996 GMC Savana van and tricked it out to suit my fancies. I gutted the interior except for the two front captain chairs, and installed a custom-made console with a hideaway cooler and drain, a PA system like I had in my high school truck, and a Rode NT1-A shock-mounted microphone on the end of a bendable arm connected to a cassette recorder that was mounted into the ceiling above the driver's seat so I could make high-end voice recordings while driving down the road. Many have been transcribed and are in this book. I spent ten grand on an Alpine amp, Tancredi equalizer, and Focal ES speakers for a top-end vintage sound system, fixed a leopard-skin couch-bed in the back, and drilled a hole in the floor to fit an oil funnel so I could take a pee without having to pull over. I named that van "Cosmo," and Ms. Hud and I hit the road.

```
I've never cared much for destinations.
The idea of landing is too finite for my
              imagination and sense of song.
Give me a direction and a sixteen-lane highway
with room to swerve and explore along the way.
  Like jazz, I prefer to see life as a river.
```

After a few months traversing the States and either sleeping on that leopard-skin bed or in a motel, Ms. Hud and I decided we were ready to commit to being road dogs, so we upgraded, purchased a twenty-eight-foot Airstream International CCD, hooked it up to the back of Cosmo, and towed our new home on the road behind us.

Now fully self-sufficient, Ms. Hud and I became what the trailer world calls "full-timers." We carved trails from Manitoba to Guatemala and forty-eight of the forty-nine reachable United States of America in between. Our compass? Wherever we wanted to go. Our schedule? Whenever we wanted to go there. Roger Clemens is pitching in New York three days from now? That's a three-day drive from Albuquerque, New Mexico, so we'll head out in the morning and make the game. There's a Cult concert in Detroit the next night? Perfect, we'll swing by for that the day after Clemens takes the bump.

I also took my meetings with film directors on the road. For instance, if I was in Utah and headed east, I would schedule my guest to fly into Boulder, Colorado, the next morning and pick them up at the local airport. Then we would drive together and discuss the project for the next seven hours until I dropped them off at the airport in Lincoln, Nebraska, for their flight home. Behind the steering wheel has always been my favorite seat, and driving the highways of America has always been my ideal office.

We went on location to Rhode Island where I got to work with Steven Spielberg on *Amistad,* a film about a slave revolt aboard a Spanish schooner in 1839 and a case that reached the Supreme Court and became notable in the abolition movement. I also made *The Newton Boys* with my old friend who gave me my first shot in this business, Richard Linklater. It was about an outlaw gang of brothers who were the most successful train and bank robbers in history. The man I portrayed was "Willis Newton," who was from my hometown of Uvalde, Texas. One of the originators of outlaw logic, he'd rather *shoot the lock than use a key any day.*

Ms. Hud and I enjoyed boondocking and the trailer park life, especially the people we met and observed along the way. For me, this was Acting and Storytelling 101, a front-row seat to real characters in real life. It was live, not Memorex; behavior, not attitude. I wrote in my diary and recorded in my mic daily.

Trailer parks are full of renegades, runaways, professional clowns, rock band guitarists, down on their luckers, wildlife lovers, 4:00 P.M. cocktailers, book readers, retired couples, single mothers, unicyclers, inventors, patteners, gardeners, dreamers, lost souls, hippies, motorheads, meth cookers, million milers, and iron your own suit at 6:00 A.M.'ers. One thing they *all* appreciate is minding their own business, and you minding yours.

"If the door's shut, don't come knockin," is one of the first rules of trailer park livin. Sure, I heard "Matthew McConaughey's staying in the park" many times, but after a few waves and head-high howdys, everyone always respected my privacy, because for the most part everyone honored trailer park rules. When they didn't, the rest of the park let them know.

On the other hand, if you *did wanna meet people,* in the words of Bobby "Thin Lizzy" Robinson at the La-Z-Daze Mobile Home Park in Quartzsite, Arizona, *Just open the hood of your truck, plenty of people'll come to help ya.*

Ms. Hud and I took our time on the road and went where we pleased when we wanted to, *keepin the shiny side high, the rubber side low, and if you ever get in a rush just leave early,* just like Robby "Cricket" McKenzie told us when we were pulling out of a creek-side trailer park in Gadsden, Alabama.

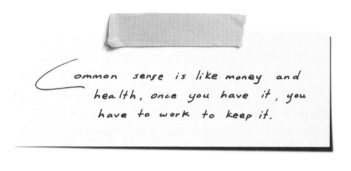

ommon sense is like money and health, once you have it, you have to work to keep it.

On one film shoot Ms. Hud and I settled into the trailer park on the Squamish Nation Indian reserve just south of the Second Narrows Bridge in Vancouver, Canada. The chief of the reservation, Mike Hunt (yes, that was his name), and I soon became buddies. Livin on the river, the Squamish were adept fishermen. But they'd become particularly efficient at the art of catching coho salmon. Instead of venturing out in their canoes with bait and hooks, they now walked into the shallow stream and simply lined up an alley of stones leading into the open entrance of an abandoned shopping cart from the local supermarket. It wasn't much of a sport, none at all really, but it was highly reliable. I would cook beef rib-eye steaks on the outdoor grill of my Airstream and trade them for coho salmon freshly captured in the steel baskets on wheels.

One day a paparazzo moved into the trailer park looking to snap pictures of me. Chief Hunt and his brothers went to him and told him he was not welcome on the reservation.

"Why?" the paparazzo asked.

"Because, we are a tribe here, and you are making one of our brothers uncomfortable."

"Well, too bad," the paparazzo defended, "I pay my rent and this is a free country!"

"Not on *this* reservation, it's not."

Chief Hunt and his brothers escorted the guy off the reservation that night. Not only did I never see him again, he never saw me—he didn't get a single photo.

Six weeks later, when I was done filming and packing up to leave, Chief Mike and his brothers gave me a parting gift, a hand-carved canoe paddle engraved with the Squamish Nation's thunderbird symbol.

"The paddle is what gives the Squamish Nation its direction on the water," Chief Hunt said. "May this one be *your* compass and watch over you on your travels, brother Matthew."

From that day on I have affectionately called my twenty-eight-foot International CCD Airstream "the Canoe."

GREENLIGHT.

LOCALIZE TO CUSTOMIZE. ADAPT TO MODIFY. THE RENAISSANCE MAN IS AT HOME WHEREVER HE GOES.

It was just after sundown somewhere along the Clark Fork River in western Montana.

I'd been driving since eight that morning, so I was pretty tired and looking for a trailer park to stretch, rest, and catch the last Pac-12 college football game on my satellite TV. With the last town too far behind me and the next one fifty miles ahead, I was in the middle of nowhere when I saw a campground sign in my headlights on the right. I immediately slowed down and took the dark dirt road off the highway.

I drove down the pitch-black pine-tree-lined trail until the path was no more. I stopped, looked around—no one, no facilities, nothing. Ms. Hud and I got out of Cosmo, the Canoe hitched behind us, to suss out the situation and look for a clue. Nothing. Then, through the pine forest, about forty yards farther into the woods I saw the small radiating orange ebb-and-flow ember of a cigarette being smoked. I killed the ignition, locked the doors, and with Ms. Hud at my side, headed for the glow.

On approach, I noticed a figure in an all-white chef's uniform, smoking, leaning against the wall, left leg straight, right knee bent, reminding me of my brother Pat back at high school. As soon as I got within earshot, the figure asked, "Lookin for a spot?"

"Yeah," I said, "with an open southern sky for my satellite dish."

Without a nudge in his stance or a pause in his puff, he motioned his head high and right. "Talk to Ed at the bar, he'll set you up."

Ms. Hud and I headed in that direction and came to a large hardwood door in the side of the same massive barnlike structure the chef was leaning against. I opened it and a wave of light, music, and revelry came blaring out. It was a tavern, and it was Saturday night. With thick enough walls to not know it until you were *in* it, the place was packed, hopping.

We stepped inside and looked for the bar when the big brown welcoming eyes of a Cheyenne barmaid bounced up and introduced herself.

"Hi, I'm Asha, come on in, anything I can get you?"

"Yeah," I said, "I'm lookin for Ed."

She nodded across the room. "That's him behind the bar over there."

I glanced up to a busy bar and then to the back of the balding, long gray-haired head behind it. "Thanks, Asha."

"Sure, need anything lemme know," she said, winking as she danced back into the fray.

Ms. Hud at my heel, we crossed to the bar.

"Hey, Ed?!" I raised my voice to get his attention over the hubbub.

"Yeah, whaddaya want?!" Ed yelled from a beer tap, barely glancing over his shoulder.

Busy serving the local crowd what he already knew they wanted, Ed wasn't looking for any *new* business tonight. He stayed with his pour.

Ed had an epileptic tic, where his face contorted and his tongue stretched out of his mouth without his choosing, but his condition had obviously done nothing to dampen his superiority as this saloon's concierge.

"A spot for my trailer with an open southern sky!" I yelled across the bar.

"A what in the sky?!" he squawked, finally turning to see who this uninvited wahoo was already asking for things that weren't on the menu.

"A spot with an open southern sky," I pointed, "so my satellite dish can get reception for the nine o'clock football game."

Now crossing to serve that beer he'd just poured, he glanced my way on his way by and said, "Nope."

"Hey, you Matthew McConaughey?" a voice to my left drunkenly asked.

Making sure to stake my ground and not appear to be an easy prey for their night's entertainment,* I answered in a semi-smartass way, "For twenty-nine years," I said. "Why?"

Too drunk to catch my dis, a big smile came across the guy's face and he said, "Shi-iit, I *knew* it!"

He grabbed my hand and shook it.

"I'm Sam, sit down and lemme buy you a drink, introduce you to my uncle Dave. He's in the shitter right now, be back in a minute."

I decided this place looked more fun than a football game, and since they weren't offering a southern sky anyway, I obliged.

"Lemme take my dog for a walk and set up my trailer, be back in thirty."

I left the bar to walk out when I heard a voice bark from the bar, "That'll be eleven bucks! Take any spot you want, they're all open." It was Ed.

Thirty minutes later I walked back in and bellied up to the bar between Sam and his uncle Dave.

"What're ya drinkin, Matthew?"

"Double Cuervo on the rocks," I said loud enough for Ed to hear, but he didn't.

"Hey, sugar," Sam said to Asha, who was passing by, "give my good friend Matthew here a triple Cuervo on the rocks, will ya, sweetie?"

"Sure thing, Sam, and you know my name's Asha, so quit bein afraid to call me by it," she said with a wink.

I looked around the place. Everybody was smiling, flirting, finishing dinner, taking shots, dancing, and playing slot machines. They'd all been here before, it seemed, and most of them for years, especially Sam.

---

* Sometimes I have to set immediate boundaries or people will take advantage of my time—signatures, pictures, phone calls to their second aunt's babysitter who is a "big fan." In this particular instance, everybody was loose and I was on their territory, so I chose to set the precedent early that I was not there for show-and-tell. If I would have amiably answered, "Yeah, how'd you know?," I would have opened the floodgates to be treated like a show pony. By giving the cutting answer I did, I let Sam, and everyone in earshot, immediately know that I was not there tonight for their entertainment. I had to give em a little yellow light so I could have my green.

"Hey, honeybun, get us another round, will ya," he flirted to another passing barmaid later.

"Three more over here, baby doll!" he said to another the next time.

I noticed that each time he called them by a general term of endearment, they each then asked him to call them by their own names instead. The girls were not threatened; they were not concerned with gender politics. If anything, they showed affection for him.

Between rounds four and five, Sam got up to go to the restroom. I asked his uncle Dave, who had been quietly sitting on the other side of me the entire night, "What's with Sam calling every barmaid 'sweetie,' 'honey,' 'baby,' or 'sugar,' and every barmaid asking him to call her by her name instead?"

Uncle Dave took a sincere swig before looking me in the eye and giving me his answer.

"Sam lost his first and only wife two weeks after they were married six years ago, and after six years of comin in here with him six nights a week, he still don't remember any of the barmaids' names. Hasn't remembered or been able to say *any* woman's name since. He can't."

Around 3:00 A.M., with the bar thinned out but the party far from over, I was rolling dice against the wall with a dozen of the late-night patrons. Josie, the tavern's hotel manager, was thirty-five years old, had crooked teeth, a receding hairline, a pair of 34-inch-waist Dickey pants leather belted around her 26-inch midsection, a loyal black Labrador by her side, and a thirteen-month-old son sleeping in the baby carriage on the floor next to her—all credit to a one-night stand she had a little over two years back when she was traveling through here just like me and met a dude named Jack in this very bar, where they proceeded to head to his hotel room and shag up for the night. When she woke up the next morning, Jack was gone but his black Lab was still bedside, so she "hung around the place for a while," and a couple months later she found out she was pregnant. Tonight, Josie was "rollin the dice for a new set of tires cus last month I drove eight miles on the flat one and ruined the other three."

Then there was Donnie, an organic mushroom farmer who was currently livin in a cabin with Donna. The drunker he got, the more sentimental and concerned he got about all the locals "thinkin he's sleepin with Donna." "*D and D,*" everyone kept teasing them. You see, Donna was married, but her man had to take a drilling job in Alaska, where he'd been working for the last year. She admitted she thought about *shaggin up* with Donnie because "He's a man, and I'm a woman," but said, "I'm just helping him out cus he don't have a place to stay and I got an extra room." Donna had two master's degrees, but "degrees don't get you too far in Montana," she said. "I work at the Humane Society fifty miles from here in Missoula all day then bartend here at night." Then she showed me the hair she'd been growing on her legs and armpits since August. "Gettin ready for winter," she said.

Bill and Susie had been married twenty-two years and ran a bar fifteen miles up the road that never paid for itself, so they retired from working altogether. Susie swore that being the mother to Bill's two teenage sons from his previous marriage was a *lot harder than making that bar stay open.* Bill said that Montana's greatest export is its kids. Primary education was excellent, and most parents were good ones, but since it was so hard to make a livin in this state, all the kids leave to find work. "But once they make enough money to get by, they *all* move back home, cus there's nothin like Montana."

Glad they didn't have a spot with an open southern sky.

GREENLIGHT.

One of the great freedoms of trailer life is that you can hitch up, leave, and find a new backyard *whenever* you want. Chase down sporting events, concerts, boondock in the desert, wake up to a grizzly bear out your window on an Idaho river morning, hike through the Antelope Valley of Utah, meet people like I did in Montana, or get a Port Authority escort through Times Square in New York City, but you also need a place to get your mail. I especially liked the Golden, Colorado, summers and the Austin, Texas, autumns, so I got a P.O. box at a park in each one. These two destinations served as "home bases" for me, two addresses where Ms. Hud and I would stop and stay awhile, read my mail, hardwire to city amps and water, hang out with old friends, and plan our next adventure.

White Collar Prayers

Ever been to a
Baptist church in
the Deep South?

They pray real
prayers.

They pray for
things they *need*.

God, if I'm sick
bring me a doctor.

God, if I'm sued
bring me a lawyer.

God, if I'm
cold bring me a
blanket.

God, if I'm hungry
bring me some
food.

**Blue Collar
Prayers.**

Then there's the
privileged pray-
ers.

They pray fake
prayers.

They pray for
things they *want*.

God, help me win
this game.

God, make momma
buy me that dress.

God, get me an
Oscar nomination.

God, let me get
that yacht.

**White Collar
Prayers.**

We need to quit
asking God to
answer *these* types
of prayers.

He's busy,

trying to get a
new set of tires.

TURN
THE PAGE

AFTER OVER THREE YEARS ON the road Ms. Hud and I started hankering for a tad more domesticity—cleaner sheets, a full kitchen, and some more water pressure sounded like Shangri-la, so I decided to rent a two-bedroom house in the sleepy little neighborhood of Tarrytown, in the heart of Austin, Texas. Besides the autumns and going to college there, I liked Austin because it always let me be myself. It's really the secret to why Austin is so cool; all you have to *be* in Austin is you, and Austin appreciates it when you are. It's never needed proof of me in a picture, it's always just been happy to see me.

Tarrytown was the kind of neighborhood where dogs ran off the leash, kids could chase a ball into the street without looking for oncoming cars, and grandparents hadn't changed their address since they were born there. I had a garden to tend to, a one hitter to hit before I did, *and* my alma mater's football season to watch. Live.

It was late Saturday afternoon in Darrell K Royal Memorial Stadium when my eighteenth-ranked Texas Longhorns had just beaten the

177

undefeated and number-three nationally ranked Nebraska Cornhuskers 24–20, handing the Huskers their only defeat of the season. The city was on fire and so was I. It was time to celebrate.

I partied through the night into Sunday, and through Sunday night without sleeping a wink.

IF YOU'RE HIGH ENOUGH, THE SUN'S ALWAYS SHINING.

At 2:30 that Monday morning, I finally decided to wind down. It was time to lower the lights, get undressed, open up the window, and let the jasmine scent from my garden come inside. It was time to smoke a bowl and listen to the beautiful African melodic beats of Henri Dikongué play through my home speakers. It was time to stand over my drum set and follow the rhythm of the blues *before* they got to Memphis, on my favorite Afro-Cuban drum born of ceremony and speaking in tongues, the congas.

For me, the congas, bongos, and djembe have always been the purest and most instinctual instruments. No sticks, no electricity, no equalizer, no strings, no tools or amendments, just skin to skin with the most analogue spoken language, prayer, and dance known to man—the percussion. The root of music, from the roots of music, Africa. It was time to lose my mind in it, take flight into the haze, and slip into the dream. It was time for a jam session.

What I didn't know was that while I was banging away in my bliss, two Austin policemen also thought *it was time* to barge into my house unannounced, wrestle me to the ground with nightsticks, handcuff me, and pin me to the floor.

"Ohhh, looky who we got here," the 'roided-up cop with a crew cut, who *looked* like a Nebraska Cornhusker himself, said as he read the driver's license he picked up off my coffee table.

Then he picked up the bong. "And looky what we got here. Mr. McConaughey, you are under arrest for disturbing the peace, possession of marijuana, and resisting arrest," he proudly stated while squatting atop me, knee in my back.

"Fuck you, motherfucker! You broke in my house! Fuck, yeah, I resisted!"

"That's enough!" he grunted, then wrangled me to my feet. "We're takin you downtown."

The other officer, the more civil one of the two, grabbed a blanket off the couch and moved to wrap it around my body.

"Ohhhh no!" I barked. "I'm not putting *shit* on! My naked ass is *proof* I was mindin my own business!"

They escorted me out of my house through the courtyard entry on the way to the street. Still naked and reluctant to submit to the inevitability of my predicament, I got relative, and decided it would be a clever idea to *run up the walls* left and right of the gated passageway and do *a somersault backflip over* the Cornhusker cop who was guiding me from behind. My thinking was that in midflight, while upside down in the air, I would *assume a pike position and then slide my cuffed wrists under my butt and up and over my legs,* then stick the landing *behind* the Cornhusker, now with my fettered hands in *front* of me. My rationale at the time was that after pulling off such an extraordinary Houdini-like stunt, the officers would be so impressed that they would abrogate the arrest and set me free. I know, stupid, but remember, I'd been celebrating for thirty-two and a half hours straight.

Whether my plan of action was physically possible or not, I'll never know. It didn't happen. Instead, *before I'd taken three steps up the wall,* the Cornhusker body slammed me back down onto the brick footpath.

Meanwhile, word must have spread over the police scanner as to just who had been arrested because there on the street were six lit-up cop cars and about forty of my neighbors.

179

"Sure you don't want this blanket?" the civil cop asked again.

"Hell no, this is *PROOF* of my innocence!!" I yelled to everyone on the block and one more over.

They lowered my head, put me in the back of the patrol car, and drove me to the precinct. After we landed and I declined the third offer to wear the blanket, we headed up the steps toward the entrance of the Austin Police Department.

At the double doors to admissions, a six-foot-six, 285-pound, tatted-up, working inmate greeted me just outside the entryway. He was holding a pair of men's orange institutional pants. Before he could say a word, I said, "Proof of my innocence, man."

He just looked at me, seeming to understand but knowing better. "We all innocent, man. Trust me, you *do* wanna put these on."

Maybe it was his honest eyes or the fact that he was a fellow offender, or maybe it was the sudden realization that, when a six-foot, six-inch jailbird built like a brick shithouse tells you *You do wanna put on some pants before you go in the clink,* it's probably best to listen.

"OK."

He dropped to his knees, opened up the pant legs, and shimmied the prison cottons up my shanks until the elastic waistband was around mine; then, I headed for the pokey.

At 9:30 A.M., my thirty-two-and-a-half-hour buzz now turned hangover, I was sitting in the corner of the cell when two people showed up on the other side of the bars.

"Mr. McConaughey, I'm Judge Penny Wilkov and this is criminal defense attorney Joe Turner." An orderly unlocked the cell door.

"I don't know how in the hell a disturbing the peace call escalated into a class A misdemeanor of resisting arrest and a class B misdemeanor of possession of less than two ounces of marijuana," the judge said, "or why two of our police officers forcibly entered your home without fair warning. I am going to dismiss the disturbing the peace and possession misdemeanors and give you a personal recognizance bond on the resisting arrest. I don't understand or agree with how this situation escalated."

"Well, Judge Penny, I'm not sure what *that* all that means, but I don't either," I said.

Joe Turner, who was the same attorney who successfully defended Willie Nelson years earlier in a possession case, spoke up. "Judge, we all agree that this situation got out of hand very quickly, but you also gotta understand that these policemen literally broke into this man's house while he was playing some bongos in his birthday suit! The resisting arrest was self-defense! I suggest you dismiss it altogether and my client will plead to the class C violation of a sound ordinance as he was indeed bangin on those bongos pretty damn loud for 2:36 in the morning."

"Deal, case closed," said the judge.

"What's *that* mean?" I asked.

Joe pulled out his wallet, grabbed a fifty-dollar bill, waved it in my face, then looked at me and said, "Means I'll pay your get-out-of-jail fee and you owe me fifty bucks, you're free to go. I got a car waitin for ya at the back entrance or you can meet the press out front, there's plenty of em waitin. Here's a bag of fresh clothes your neighbor dropped off for ya."

I thanked them both, got dressed in the lavatory, splashed my face with cold water, and tried to breathe out the blues that were starting to set in. Why the blues, you ask? Well, obviously I was lucky, walking out of jail only $50 poorer—this didn't happen to everyone who got hauled in on charges like resisting arrest and marijuana possession. The problem was, as I've said, in my family, we didn't get in trouble for *committing* the crime, **we got in trouble for getting caught.** I wasn't raised to end up in jail, for anything or *any* amount of time, and even though my offense was one I'd committed many times before and would many times more, I got caught, and for that, I felt guilty. Outlaw logic.

Looking for some fearless consolation, I decided to call my mom before I chose which way to leave my first prison stint. Maybe it was the fact that while I was sure she would have no mercy for my circumstance, at the same time I knew she would pour a drink and toast to how it was I got into it. Was it going to be *her* that answered or was it going to be that new groupie fan? I didn't know. Turns out it was both.

"They *what,* Matthew?! Broke into your house!? Those son of a bitches, you keep your head up," she said. "There is *nothing* wrong with smokin a little fun stuff and playing your drums naked at night in your own home; who do they think they are comin in your house like that?!"

Just what I needed. I hung up and decided to stride toward the media mob out front instead of sneaking out the back.

GREENLIGHT.

Two days later, BONGO NAKED T-shirts were all over Austin.

I framed that "violating the sound ordinance" ticket.

The "Cornhusker" was later dismissed from the force.

Joe Turner got the resisting arrest expunged from my file and I got my virginity back, turning my life of crime around.

But my two-day party had other consequences.

With the help of an editor of the local newspaper, who carelessly printed a picture of my house *with* the address on the front page of the Metro section, my residence in Tarrytown quickly became a tourist attraction, even for the locals. Good-hearted people dropped off six-packs of beer, different kinds of drums, and a lot of weed. It was amusing and kind, but it turned our sleepy little neighborhood street into South Bundy Drive in Brentwood. No more leashless dogs or chasing bouncing balls into the street without looking.

Fame can change people, but in this case, it changed a place. My anonymity gone again, it wasn't fair to me or my neighbors for me to live there any longer as the peace I had found on Meadowbrook Drive was now disturbed. They all heavily protested my evacuation, but I had no choice. Time for goodbyes instead of see you laters. Ms. Hud and I packed our bags, ducked out of the lease, and headed west again.

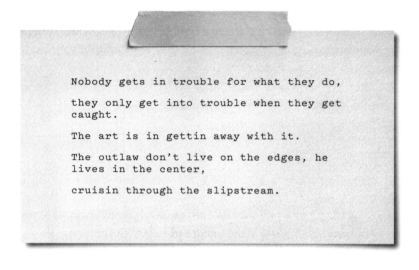

Nobody gets in trouble for what they do, they only get into trouble when they get caught.

The art is in gettin away with it.

The outlaw don't live on the edges, he lives in the center,

cruisin through the slipstream.

January 2000. With an actor's strike looming and a few films since my last box office hit, I needed to get back to Hollywood and start the hustle again anyway. I needed to be in the industry's eyeline, work the town, take meetings, be around the creatives that were making the decisions.

Neither the box office performance of *The Newton Boys, Contact, Amistad, EdTV,* and *U-571,* nor my performances in them met or raised the white-hot expectations of *Matthew McConaughey* in the movie industry since *A Time to Kill.* The first-class dramatic studio offers I was looking for were no longer being offered. I was still a bankable star but my shine had dimmed, I'd lost some *heat* as the industry calls it, and I was losing my hair.

With the strike imminent and Hollywood scrambling to start as many productions as possible before a walkout, I got an *above my market value* cash offer to play the lead opposite Jennifer Lopez in *The Wedding Planner.* I read the script, it looked like fun, the money was generous, and I was ready to work. Shooting started in two weeks in downtown Hollywood. I said yes, and Ms. Hud and I made our new address the legendary Chateau Marmont in the heart of Tinseltown. Yes, where Led Zeppelin's John Bonham rode his hog through the lobby and John Belushi OD'd on coke in Bungalow 3.

Ready to rock 'n' roll, congas in tow, I cashed that healthy check from the studio, bought a pair of leather pants and a Triumph Thunderbird motorcycle, wrote the Chateau a running tab of 120 grand, and got a key to my room until whenever I turned it in.

Acting in a romantic comedy was different from anything I'd done before. Engineered to be *light,* not lightweight, they are built for buoyancy and I learned to enjoy skipping from cloud to cloud as one needs to do in order to keep these types of films afloat. I quickly realized that, unlike in dramatic acting, you cannot *drop anchor* and *hang your hat on humanity* in a rom-com, lest you sink the ship. I enjoyed this kind of acting, it was all greenlights, like a *Saturday character* in a story that was a series of Saturdays.

Back at the Chateau it was always a Saturday, easy street, and I was *on* it, once again, having committed to *my man.* Now, eager to dance with my devils instead of fight them, I was keen to negotiate the abyss, broker a deal with lack of restraint, and see if I could come out the other side unscathed.

My days of it'd be rude not to and I don't have to, so I will, led to many a morning of I don't knows and let's not remembers. You know how it is, when you're up to nothin no good's usually next.

Single, healthy, honest, and eligible, I enjoyed the transience of a high-class hotel that promoted mischief: transactions; flings; affairs; renting to rent, not to own. I wore the leathers. I rode the Thunderbird. I took a lot of showers in the daylight hours, rarely alone. I partook.

I embraced the fun, my fame, and the curfewless hours. When I wasn't working, I'd read scripts tanning by the pool, write poetry, have a friend over for lunch, take Ms. Hud for a walk, go for a run, then get ready to saunter into the Hollywood lights. My life being designed for ease, these nightly adventures could take place *on foot,* which was a perk considering my affection for liberal libations. I'd meet friends for dinner and ultimately return to the Chateau for late-night revelry of song, dance, and the occasional wrestling match. Localizing and customizing once again, I also had a key to the hotel's kitchen, which I conveniently used to find and cook 3:00 A.M. steaks.

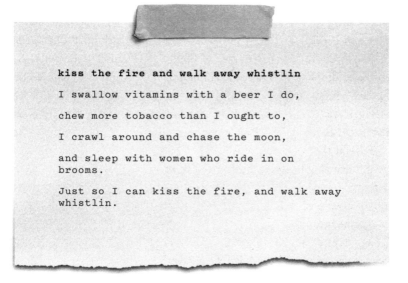

kiss the fire and walk away whistlin

I swallow vitamins with a beer I do,

chew more tobacco than I ought to,

I crawl around and chase the moon,

and sleep with women who ride in on brooms.

Just so I can kiss the fire, and walk away whistlin.

Then I got offered the role of Denton Van Zan in the film *Reign of Fire*. Van Zan was a cigar-gnawing, apocalyptic badass dragon slayer who ate the heart of every dragon he slayed and carried a dwarf around on his shoulder. The *dwarf on the shoulder* part later got cut out of the script but I always loved it. I immediately had an understanding and a need for a character like Van Zan. A man with a singular constitution, alone, not doing what he could to survive, rather doing everything he could to deny extinction. An island of a man whose freedom was his isolation.

Maybe it was the eighteen-month hedonism tour I'd been on at the Chateau—the booze, the women, the gluttony. Maybe it was an aggressive recoil to distance myself from the bubbly mendacities of my recent rom-com emasculation. Maybe it was both and then some. Either way, I felt like it was time to earn my Saturdays again. I needed some yellow lights.

I'd been questioning my own existence, and searching for meaning in my own life for as long as I could remember, but now, for the first time, I was also questioning the existence of God. An existential crisis? I'd call it an existential challenge, and one I was up for. I didn't as much cease *believing in God* as much as I doubled down on self-reliance and the responsibility of my free will. I was done with the excuses that fate allows, I was ready to be the boss of me, the one to blame *and* acquit, I needed to own that it was *my* hands on the steering wheel.

Tired of letting myself off the hook on easy street, I was done with unearned forgiveness, feigned compassion, the protocol of manners and graces, and self-indulgent sentiment. Livin for tomorrow when we might just all be racing to the red light seemed like a fool's errand. Brave enough to say it's on me and me only in my prayers, but still scared enough to keep praying, I gave credit to the notion that it might *all be for nothing,* and I quit *doing it for something.*

"If you are there, God," I prayed, "I hope you appreciate a man who won't retreat from the sweat it takes to gain self-determination. I hope you will reward a man who has decided to quit hiding behind the fatal blind belief that it's all in your hands."

Van Zan's boots were my size; I was ready to wear them.

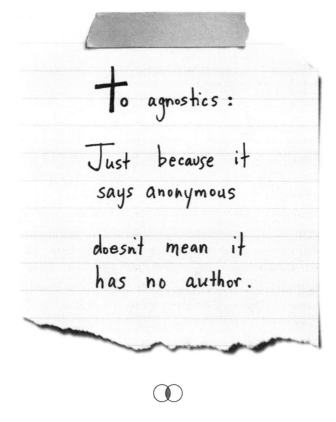

To agnostics :

Just because it says anonymous

doesn't mean it has no author.

I accepted the offer and immediately shaved my head. Why? Well, I could tell you that it was my *vision* for the character or that I knew if I did it would piss off the studio and I was looking for a fight, but really it was about the fact that, like I said, I was losing my hair.

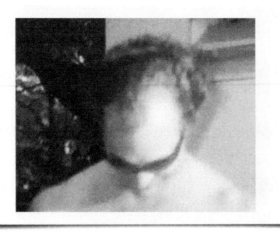

I had recently gotten turned on to a hair restoration product called Regenix that required twice-a-day topical applications. I also had read that a good skull shave can improve the chances of thicker regrowth, so, being a man who appreciates the value of vanity, if I was playing Van Zan, he was going to have a shaved head.*

I don't know if you've ever shaved *your* head before, but if you have, you know it can be gnarly under there. I had dents in my cranium, a psoriasis patch, and my scalp was chalk white. The paparazzi got a shot of my freshly shaved nugget the day after I did it, and that photo was in *People* magazine the next week.

Soon enough, my phone rang.

"You did *not* shave your head," an ominous whispering voice stated. For the sake of his privacy I'll leave his name off the page, but he was a top studio executive with a very large financial investment in *Reign of Fire*.

---

* After an aboriginal handshake with a friend that *guarantees what two people agree on will happen if they both believe it* and two years of diligently applying Regenix to my scalp daily, my hairline returned better than ever, and it all started with a good head shave.

"Yes, I did," I said bluntly.

"No, you didn't, I refuse to believe this, Matthew. You just wore a bald cap as a prank." Again *stating* not asking.

"No . . . I *shaved* my head."

He hung up.

That afternoon the front desk delivered a handwritten letter to my room.

> *In our talk this morning, Mr. McConaughey, you refused to admit that you had in fact not shaved your head.*
>
> *If you are in denial of this fact please come clean so we can proceed on the journey of making this film together.*
>
> *If, in fact, it* is *true that you shaved your head, this would be a tragedy, a major mis-step, and an act that May bring you very <u>bad karma</u>.*

Yes, he underlined and put in bold print, "**<u>bad karma</u>**."

Well, I thought, *I oughta kick this guy's ass for throwin the karma shade but the shaved head sounds like a real dealbreaker.* Hmmm. That fight I was looking for? Got it.

I'd learned a few things about the Hollywood hustle over the years. For starters, it's better to play your own game in the business of Hollywood than to do your business playing Hollywood's game. You have to *get the joke,* and the joke is, nothing's personal. From the *I love you*s to the unreturned phone calls when your last picture didn't perform, they will pick you up in a limo, but you might have to catch a cab home. It's not personal, it's just business.

That bad karma threat? It wasn't personal, but it *was* arrogant, cavalier, and in very poor taste. It was time to trump his gesture.

superstitions

The other day I went in a roadside quikmart

and bought a candy bar and a beer.

The total came up $6.66 on the register

so I paid the cashier.

And left a penny in the "need one take one,
got one give one" saucer.

There was a big Hollywood industry party coming up that weekend. All the top executives and bigwigs would be there, and most likely Mr. Bad Karma as well.

I bought a custom-cut three-piece Gucci blue suit that matched my eyes. I tanned my pale head poolside for four hours a day for the next five days, then I greased my now beautifully browned scalp with some oil, not of Mink, until it was so shiny it would have made Dwayne Johnson jealous. Then I went to that party.

I didn't see Bad Karma. I didn't have to. People noticed, especially the ladies. And people noticed them noticing me.

The following Monday my phone rang again. Bad Karma calling.

"It scared me at first, but I've had a change of heart, Matthew. I *love* the shaved head! You look original. And so handsome! I love it."

I put a penny in the saucer.

GREENLIGHT.

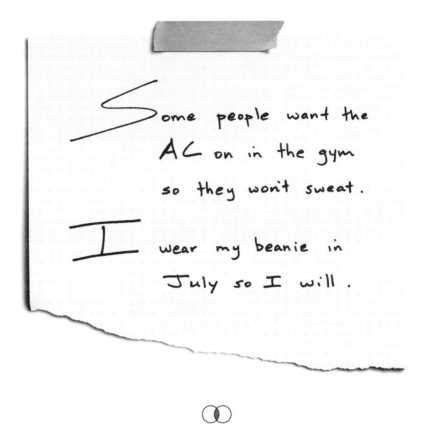

Some people want the AC on in the gym so they won't sweat. I wear my beanie in July so I will.

I had two months to prepare and train to become *my man*, Van Zan. I needed isolation so I decided to go out to my brother's ranch, Loca-Pelotas, in West Texas, seventeen miles outside of the nearest town of 518 people. Very secluded, fifteen hundred acres, hot as hell in the middle of summer—a perfect place to prepare to slay dragons. Next up was devising my own original dragon slayer mind, body, and spirit daily workout regime. What would a dragon slayer do? How would a dragon slayer train?

I made a plan that would be executed in the mid-July 108-degree weather:

1) **TAKE A DOUBLE SHOT OF TEQUILA EVERY MORNING AT SUNRISE BEFORE I GET OUT OF BED.** Yeah, a dragon slayer would do that. Have fire breath to beat the fire breather, get the insides on fire first thing to start the day. To beat a dragon, be a dragon. Perfect.

2) **RUN FIVE MILES ACROSS THE DESERT DAILY, BAREFOOT. TWO AND HALF MILES OUT, TWO AND HALF MILES BACK.** Yeah, toughen up the soles of my feet. I've got tender feet now, I wear shoes. I've got to toughen up the soles of my feet. Plus, dragons have tough skin and I have to become more like my prey, yeah, a dragon slayer like Van Zan would have tough soles, ward off infection. Brilliant.

3) **KEEP MY HEART RATE BELOW 60 WHILE STANDING ON THE EDGE OF THE BARN'S ROOFTOP OVERLOOKING A FORTY-FOOT DROP ONTO THE CONCRETE BELOW.** Yeah, I'm afraid of heights, but Van Zan wouldn't be. I'll do it every day until I can stand on my heels with my feet over the edge while holding a resting heart rate in the low 50s. Yeah, that's what I'll do. Fuckin aces.

4) **RUN OUT INTO THE PASTURES EVERY NIGHT AT MIDNIGHT AND TACKLE SLEEPING COWS.** Yeah, I'm gonna full-on tackle cows, knock em off their feet, I'll get thick, burly, strong, yeah, that's what a dragon slayer would do. That's what Van Zan would do. Deal.

So, how did it go?

Well, on the sixth morning I gagged up the double Cuervo shot that was awaiting me bedside at sunrise. Then again on morning seven. Bad idea. Done.

At midnight on my ninth day a large bull headbutted me and gave me a concussion as I tried to wrestle him to the ground. Oops.*

---

* One night the ranch manager, a seventy-year-old man from Mexico, heard a herd of cows get spooked and came out of his cabin to see why. That's when he saw my naked ass in the middle of them. That's how the ranch got the name LocaPelotas, meaning "crazy balls" in Spanish.

After eleven days of running five miles barefoot across the rocky, 108-degree hot desert sand and stones, oyster-sized blisters formed on the bottoms of my feet so big and so bubbled that I couldn't even walk, much less run. Uh-oh.

And after two months of trying, I never got closer than three feet from the edge of that barn's rooftop, and even then my heart rate never got lower than 125. Nice try.

My *dragon slayer workout regime* had failed miserably, but the upside was that I experienced a lot of pain, as any good dragon slayer would.

With my self-inflicted sixty-day dragon slayer boot camp complete, I headed to Ireland to make the movie. Van Zan was a blast to inhabit— a warrior without a country and bald with a battle-ax. I miss him. Great characters earn my respect and Van Zan was one who didn't so much get the madness *out* of my system as he made me own more of my own. He elevated my expectations of what it takes to survive and reminded me that duty is worth more than the vanities of a home field advantage. His tomahawk still hangs on the wall behind my back in my office today.

After wrapping four months of filming in the wet and cold Irish winter I was physically and mentally exhausted, and pleased to finally get some rest and mend my bruised and battered body and mind. Spiritually, I was strong; challenging my reliance on God's existence in order to rely more on my own was proving a valuable practice. Like the time when my dad moved on, I practiced being *less impressed, more involved* once again.

It was three days after completing principal photography, and I was getting some much-needed sleep one night in the Morrison Hotel on the north side of the Liffey River in Dublin, Ireland, when . . .

I HAD A WET DREAM.

I was floating downstream on my back in the Amazon River. Wrapped up by anacondas and pythons. Surrounded by crocodiles, piranhas, and a few freshwater sharks. There were African tribesmen lined up shoulder to shoulder on the ridge to the left of me as far as my eyes could see.

I was at peace.

Eleven frames.

Eleven seconds.

Then I came.

Again.

Yes, the exact same wet dream I had had *five* years earlier.

I was sure about two things in the dream. One, I was on the *Amazon* River and two, those were *African* tribesmen on the ridge.

It was a sign.

Having already been to the Amazon and physically proven that it was, in fact, located in the continent of South America, I knew it was now time to go to Africa. But where in Africa?

A couple of nights later, while cross-examining the African atlas, wondering where in this massive continent the wet dream was calling me to, I was listening to one of my favorite musicians, Ali Farka Touré.

Then it came to me. Ali is known as the *African Bluesman.*

Where's he from? I hopped from the couch to grab the CD case with the liner notes. "Niafunké, Mali," north of Mopti on the Niger River.

"I'll go find *him*," I said.

It was time to chase down the other half of my wet dream.

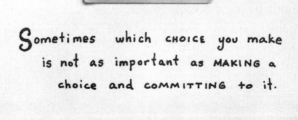

Sometimes which CHOICE you make is not as important as MAKING a choice and COMMITTING to it.

I got a one-way ticket to Bamako, the capital of Mali, then hitchhiked nine hours to the port city of Mopti, where I met a guide named Issa who had a boat. I introduced myself as "David" for anonymity's sake and told him I was looking for Ali Farka. We set sail upriver toward Niafunké the next day.

After a four-day trip up the Niger River in a small, four-horsepower outboard-motored dugout canoe called a pirogue, I arrived at the small river town of Niafunké, where after five hours of searching, I found Ali at his second wife's house. He had no idea who I was other than a traveler from America who was a fan. His second wife prepared lunch for us and we ate in the traditional Malian way, sitting on the floor in a circle around a communal bowl of seasoned rice, serving ourselves with our right hand, never the left.*

---

* In the Muslim religion, the left hand is the one you wipe your backside with.

Ali was one of my musical heroes but he was also, unbeknownst to him, my journey's only port of call on the second-largest landmass on earth. The lone geographical coordinate I chose to chase in my dream: 15°55'55.92"N, 3°59'26.16"W (the longitude and latitude of Niafunké).

What sign would my stop with him give me that might lead me to the meaning of the *African tribesmen lined up along the left ridge of my Amazon River wet dream?* We ate, he played me some of his songs, and Issa translated my passion for his music in the local dialect, Bambara. Later I asked him, "Why do you only perform in West Africa and France, why do you not tour in other countries, including America?" He solemnly answered.

"Because there I would be dried shit, neither me
nor my scent would stick with you.

Here, I am wet shit, both me and my
scent stick with you."

At the end of the day we hugged our goodbyes, then Issa and I returned to the pirogue, destination unknown. *Now what? Where does the dream want me to go from here?* I thought. Without any solicitation from me, Issa began to speak.

"There is a magical people in Mali called the Dogon. They have an extraterrestrial transmission of knowledge of the cosmological facts of the stars that they knew long before the development of modern astronomy. They fled to a place called the Bandiagara Escarpment to escape the Muslim invasion over one thousand years ago where they now live in villages along the river's edge. I think this is a good place for you to go to, Daouda ("David" in Bambara), a place you will *remember*," he said.

Another celestial suggestion.

Remember, I thought, *better to have a scent and be remembered, than to have none and be forgotten.* That's it. *Wet shit.* "Yes, let's go *there*," I said.

We loaded the pirogue and headed up the Niger for a five-day journey, first north, then south to chase down the rest of my wet dream.

On the way to the Bandiagara, we stopped in the legendary town of Timbuktu. A center for art and learning, it is a quiet little trade settlement situated just north of the Niger River on the south side of the Sahara Desert.

One night, after an afternoon of racing camels in the Sahara, Issa, two of his well-educated friends, Ali (not Farka Touré) and Amadou, and I were finishing dinner on the veranda of the hotel restaurant when a pretty young lady about twenty-five years of age came strolling through, having a solicitous *look* at each table full of males. It was obvious she was a lady of the night and was trolling for business.

"Oh, this is, this is not good," said Ali. "This is a Muslim woman, and this is *not* the Muslim way. You do not go and sell your body, this is a disgrace, she should *not* be doing this."

"Well," Amadou countered, "it is not for any of us to judge what someone should or should *not* be doing. We do not know her particular circumstances, what she *does* or does *not* is not for us to say."

The two men went back and forth in this conversation, which grew increasingly animated, passionate, and loud. In what appeared to me to be an argument, I interjected at the first pause in their discussion.

"I agree with Ali. It is *not* what she should be doing. She is young and has her health, she should be putting out more effort to have a respectable job rather than choosing prostitution at her young and able age. I believe Ali is right, I think—"

Just then, Ali, the guy *whose side I was agreeing with,* snapped at me,

"It is not about right or wrong. It is 'Do you understand?!'"

Slightly stunned, I leaned back in my chair sheepishly as Ali stared at me with sobering vengeance.

At last, Amadou, *whose side I was against,* looked at me and asked kindly, "Do you understand *that?*"

I did. "Yeah," I said, "I do, sorry."

To which Amadou just as sharply and still holding my gaze said,

"You'd better be different, not sorry."

Wow, he'd just recited to me a version of what I'd said to myself in Australia when I'd refused to call the Dooleys *Mum* and *Pop.* A double whammy of African proverbs: They are not trying to win arguments of right or wrong. They are trying to understand each other. That's different. (Hey, America, we could learn from this.) The next morning we continued toward the Bandiagara Escarpment.

A Dogon village in the Bandiagara is made up of a small cluster of mud huts. Each settlement is spaced about eight to fifteen miles apart along the river's edge. Upon arrival, the chief greets you at the encampment's border where, if he likes what he sees in your eyes, he welcomes you in. If not, you keep walking. I was always welcomed.

Having just come off filming *Reign of Fire,* I had a shaved head, a big beard, and was in sturdy physical shape. Upon coming to Mali I told Issa and anyone who asked me that I was a writer and a boxer by profession. With no electricity in the Bandiagara, nobody recognized me from my movies, and they were not very interested in me being *a writer.* They were, however, *very* interested in the *boxer* part.

Word started preceding my appearance in each village: "*Strong white man named Daouda is walking these parts.*" One day, after I showed up at a beautiful village called Begnemato, exhausted from the fourteen-mile hike to get there, I lay down on the ground to stretch my legs. Two young men soon approached, stood above me, and started talking *at* me, not *to* me, a challenge in their tone. A crowd began to gather.

"What is it they say?" I asked Issa, who sat near.

"They say they are the champion wrestlers of the village and want to challenge *strong white man named Daouda* to a match."

I continued to stretch on the ground, measuring the situation, when suddenly, the two young men ran away in opposite directions as the crowd worked into a frenzy. I looked up, and now standing above me was a large shirtless man, much more able-bodied than the two before him, with a burlap bag roped around his waist. He pointed down at my chest, then to his own, then off to his right. The crowd amplified another notch. I turned my head to have a look at what he was referring to, where I saw *more* excited villagers, all surrounding a Big. Dirt. Pit.

I then glanced at Issa.

199

He smiled. "This is Michel, he is the *re-aaal* champion wrestler of the village."

My heart began racing, the crowd roared. That's when I heard my own voice whisper in my ear, *Take the challenge or you will forever regret not knowing. Leave your scent.* Slowly, I got to my feet. Now standing eye to eye with Michel, I raised my right arm and pointed at *his* chest, then back at *my* own. Then I turned and walked toward the Big. Dirt. Pit. The villagers went apeshit.

Some people look for an excuse to DO. Others look for an excuse NOT to.

I'd always been a fan of wrestling. I followed the WWF as a kid and had decent leverage skills defending myself as the youngest brother of three, but this was different. I was in the middle of rural Africa, ninety-five miles from the nearest telephone line, standing in a Big. Dirt. Pit. in front of a well-built native African man wearing a burlap sack for pants. What were the rules? Could you *strike, bite, fight till the last man is standing*? I didn't know but was about to find out.

Michel and I stood face-to-face, the chief of the village circling us. A bead of sweat began to run down the back of my neck when Michel swung his right arm to my left hip and secured his hand to my shorts, then he looked me in the eyes and nodded. I took this to mean I should do the same, so I did, and got a firm grip on the left side of his roped waist. He then grabbed a handful of my shorts on the right side of my waist, I mirrored his move. Our faces now inches apart, the crowd decibels rising once again, Michel lowered his forehead into the soft spot just below my neck above my collarbone, and burrowed his brow in. I followed suit. Both our arms attached to the other's waist, our foreheads bored into the shoulder girdles of the other, ear to ear, we began to back our feet *away* from each other into an interlaced horizontal plank position, then dug our feet into the sand to get anchored. All I could see were two tree trunk thighs bulging in front of me, braced for attack. The chief rested his hands on our heads like a baptism, then, as he quickly lifted them, he yelled "Taht!," which I correctly took to mean "*Ding ding.*"

Round 1. Head-to-head we spun in a few circles measuring the other's might before Michel lifted me up and *into* him, my chest to his face, then body-slammed me to the ground, knocking the wind out of me. One for him. The crowd howled as he quickly mounted to try and pin me. On my back, I swiveled, trying to evade his grip, then I whipped my hips upward and swung my right leg over his head and back under his chin, and slammed his head backward to the dirt. One for me. For three to four minutes we circled, flipped, and smashed each other to the ground, but neither of us was able to pin the other. Finally, the chief stepped between us and broke up the battle. Dripping sweat, now hyperventilating, I raised my hands over my head to try and catch my breath. Blood ran from my neck, mixing with shards of my beard that had been ripped away from my face in the friction, my knees and ankles bleeding. Michel, with barely a glaze of sweat on him, stood upright staring me down, not a happy man. That's when the chief held two fingers to the sky and the crowd pushed the limits of hysteria even further.

Face-to-face in the middle of the ring again we took our positions. Hands to hips, heads burrowed, ear to ear, we dug in and let the baptism begin again, "Taht!!"

Round 2. Back home in Texas my advantage as a wrestler was always my strong legs and ass. Here in a Big. Dirt. Pit. in Africa opposite Michel I was reminded that I was no longer in Texas. More aggressive out of the gate this round, Michel immediately came on the attack. I slipped his first takedown and drove him to the ground

face-first; mounting him from behind, I employed the reverse of one of my favorite WWF childhood moves, the Boston Crab.[*]

Just when I thought I'd exhausted him, he somehow flipped me off his back and the next thing I knew I was gasping for air, leg locked between his tree trunk stumps. Now seeing stars, I fought to twirl my hips and release his latched ankles. With Michel's legs still locked around my waist, I managed to climb to my feet, his arms bracing him from the ground. I twisted and turned until I felt one of his sweaty legs lose its grip and begin to slide around my stomach. *This* was my chance. His death clench now weakened, I pushed his legs downward, slipped

---

[*] The Boston Crab is a professional wrestling hold where the wrestler has his opponent facedown and pulls his opponent's legs upward so that his opponent's back and legs are bent back toward his own head. In my instance, I pulled Michel's head upward so that his back and head were bent back toward his own legs. A Boston Crab, in reverse, as in the picture above.

out of his squeeze, and dove on top of him, where I got my left arm around his neck and fought to set a headlock. Unable to establish it but still maintaining leverage, I remained coiled up with him on the dirt until we were both absolutely exhausted, a stalemate. That's when the chief stepped in and called it. We slowly got to our feet and the chief escorted us to the middle of the Big. Dirt. Pit. where he *raised both our hands* to the sky in victory. The crowd wailed.

Both of us sweaty and spent, but only me a bloody mess, Michel and I were peering at each other in postfight regard when he lowered his eyes and suddenly bolted out of the ring and sprinted away from the village. The crowd, which now included *everyone* in the village, enveloped me with chants of "Daouda! Daouda! Daouda!"

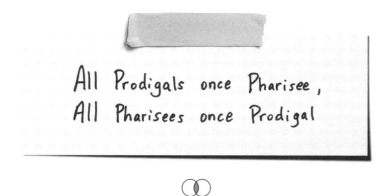

All Prodigals once Pharisee,
All Pharisees once Prodigal

That night, alone on a straw mattress, I lay on the roof of a mud hut in the Dogon village of Begnemato in the middle of Mali, Africa, staring into the heavens where I counted twenty-nine shooting stars cascade across the sky. Dreaming with my eyes open, I watched as the constellation of the Southern Cross revealed itself to me for the first time. Like the radiance of the luminescent cluster of butterflies I'd come upon on the Peruvian trail to the Amazon, I was now in the cradle of another truth. It was Divine Intervention, an *extraterrestrial transmission of cosmological facts* indeed. A *celestial suggestion?* More like a direct ordinance from God and I was the chosen one in his church. *Remember this,* I avowed.

All because I *chased down a wet dream,* literally.

GREENLIGHT.

As I began serenely dozing off into my dreams of superior sanctity, my peaceful breathing was casually interrupted by a blocked nasal passage, my own. I sat up and snorted a healthy amount of mucus into my mouth, then readied to hurl the sizable mass of coagulated phlegm off the rooftop.

Fhluuup!

The launched loogie made it no more than five inches from my curled tongue before it boomeranged back and straddled its oyster-sized snotball across my face.

I'd forgotten about the mosquito net I had put on my head earlier.

Unbelievable.

Nothing will bring you back down to earth like spitting a loogie in your own face.

Believe it.

un·be·liev·a·ble | ˌən·bə·ˈlēv·ə·b(ə)l |

adjective

not able to be believed; unlikely to be true:

so great or extreme as to be difficult to believe; extraordinary

Not able to be believed.

What a foolish word. A rude and disrespectful word. We think we use it to flatter and give credit to: "What an unbelievable play." "What an unbelievable film." "What an unbelievable act of courage." "What an unbelievable sunset." "What an unbelievable break."

Why would we define things that are incredible and awesome, things that actually make us *believe* in them more, with this pillar of antonymy? Something spectacular, phenomenal, outstanding, and most excellent, is most definitely *not, unbelievable*.

Awe-inspiring, magnificent, prodigious, and extraordinary? Yes. It just happened, you just witnessed it, you did it, *believe* it. *Un*believable? Quite the opposite. Give incredible more credit.

A man flies a suicide jet into the World Trade Center, the coronavirus comes, hurricanes ravage, fires burn, Enron's a scam, the government lies to us, our best friend lies to us, we lie to our self, our fiancée says "I do," our child says his first words, we find a cure for cancer one day, we die in peace. *Un*believable? No. It just happened, you just witnessed it, you did it, believe it.

Acknowledge the existence of greatness and phenoms, excellence and extraordinaries, pleasures and pains. Recognize them as true entities, both beautiful *and* horrible, tragic and heaven-sent. Be not naïve to awe-inspiring feats of good or good fortune, nor gullible to mankind's capacity for evil. Be not blind to the credence of natural beauties and disasters. Nothing God or Mother Nature does is *unbelievable, and if there's one thing you can depend on people being, it is people*.

Don't act so surprised, unbelievable happens all the time, sometimes it's divine, and sometimes it's a loogie in our face. Don't deny it. Depend on it, expect it.

Believe it.

● MDM on Austin Statesman movie critic ~~Chris Garcia~~ "a cynical deconstructionalist who uses big words and careless innuendo to impress himself. Because he has no point of view, he has trouble recognizing one, so he chooses to stroke himself into dorkdom."

✻ how about 2 camels on Locopolotas?

✝ RELIGION : to bind together again... (the true Latin definition: "re"-again, "ligare"-bind)

8 don't act like one, be one ... on acting, travelling

✝ the capacity for paradox is the measure of spiritual strength and the surest sign of maturity. (R. Johnson : Own Shadow" p. 78). both are true.

✝ while contradiction is static and unproductive, paradox makes room for grace and mystery... j.k.livin, 8 lane highways, maxims as bookends. (no "g" on livin)

⇕ we are the inheritors of two myths that surfaced in the 12th century.
   i) The Grail Myth - the relationship of individuality and the spiritual quest.
      (MDM on experiences and autonomy.)
   2) Tristan & Iseult - the power of romantic love.   (R. Johnson)

✛ language rich in verbs are most powerful. (The mandorla, motion, the river, life
language built on nouns is weak. (secular, polar, self-righteous
if you rely on adjectives and adverbs you have lost your way (luxury, semantics
THE VERB IS THE HOLY GROUND, THE PLACE OF THE MANDORLA   (R. Johnson)

⊕ ←"mandorla" - it unifies opposites .. binds together ... religion · where light and dark touch.
          - the middle ... peacemaking ..

Θ - heaven ⎱ poetry that "this" is "that" .. heaven is earth.
  earth ⎰

• Norby has a mandorla on his ass before he knows what to call it.
• MATTHEW 6:22 "if thy eye be single, thy whole body shall be filled with light."
• i am vain, already thinking how to use these truths autonomously .. to tatoo, to impress, to activate ... before i have slept on their enlightenment or even turned the page. but i like it.

• Mandorlas have no place for remorse or guilt. It asks for conscious work not self-indulgence.

• guilt is a cheap substitute for paradox.

• guilt is arrogant. It means we have taken sides and are sure we are right.

• to lose the power of confrontation is to lose one's chance at unity. To miss the mandorla

∿ the <u>blackmarket</u> is what i deal with.. just get in with the best <u>MAVERICKS</u> ~ the gov't does not "work" with "these people. The wealth is not shared with the common folk. so individuals must be entrepreneurs and you get "offered" everything ... at dinner, at every tour, # exchange, ferry ride, everywhere ... it is the "wild wild east" ~ salesmen at every turn. it is part of the fun.

• CD "Adama Yalomba" ~ new Malian band.

☆ TIPS for travel ~ season, outskirts, guide

⚓ the MANDORLA is not the greyness of neutrality and compromise; it is the place of the peacock's tail and rainbows. (R. Johnson)
        grace, mystery

⚜ the mandorla experience is brief. (signs, serendipity, epiphany, deja vu', truth....) and joyful. it is only a momentary glimpse... then we quickly return to the world of ego-shadow confrontation. (there is no cultural utopia to return to... There is only a religious mandorla to try and maintain on the inside... why it takes work ... daily... and work to become the truths that are revealed from the travels alone and solitude.

⚙ in Djenne at Issa's newly married friends house. All the guys are hanging out from 8:00AM to 8pm for one week after the marriage. One guy is in charge of the married guy and one girlfriend for the lady. A week to relax and have fun, celebrate the marriage and happiness so that if/when at later date when there is a hard time and unhappiness, the friends will be there to <u>remind</u> the couple of the happy time.

⇕ in the middle of all the socializing, smokin, card playin, tea makin good time, if somebody wants to kneel on the mat and pray, all they have to do is "wave off" whoever may be on the mat. The others carry on just as enthusiastically as before

The next morning I packed my rucksack and said goodbyes to my new friends before heading out on the fifteen-mile hike to the next village. At the perimeter of Begnemato a man stood waiting for me; it was Michel. Without a spoken word he gently put his palm in mine as I approached and proceeded to walk with me the full fifteen miles to the next village, holding my hand the entire way. When we arrived, he released me, silently turned around, and walked the fifteen miles back to Begnemato alone.

Later that night I said to Issa, "I have to talk to you about yesterday's wrestling match. How did I do? I think I held my own."

Issa chuckled to himself then said, "No, no, no, Daouda. You did *very* well. Everybody think Michel going to have strong white man named Daouda on his back in no more than *ten* seconds!"

"Really?" I asked.

"Yes, really. Michel not only champion of *this* village, Michel champion of *this* village and three villages *back*!!"

"Ha! So I won? That's why the village all chanted my name afterward?"

"It is not about win or lose, it is about do you accept the challenge,"

Issa said as he looked at me and smiled. "When you did that, you already won."

"You come back, Daouda, we make *money*."

I did go back. Five years later. Michel had four kids and a busted hip by then so we didn't have another wrestling match, but he still held my hand and walked me the fifteen miles to the village the next day. Wet shit, I had left my scent.*

GREENLIGHT.

---

* In 2015, Issa came to America for the first time and stayed with us for three weeks. We vacationed together in Greece last year.

the justice it deserves

To appreciate a place fully, a man must
know that he can live there.

When all his discomforts disappear and
he lets himself be owned by the place.

He needs to customize and localize
himself to the place he visits,

to the degree that he *knows* he could
dwell there forever.

Then and only then, is it truly
acceptable for him to leave.

Wherever you are, give the place the
justice it deserves.

I came back to Los Angeles a changed man again, feeling more clear and practical than I ever had. I gave my wet dream *and* the people it took me to the justice *they* deserved, and my justifications were more than returned. Another period of twenty-two days with very limited spoken English and mostly pantomimed conversations gave me a solitary yet communal experience that made me feel more at home than I ever had before, and I got my wink back. With my tolerance for verbose vanities not far above zero, I knew the reentry into my fast-paced and privileged life back in Hollywood was going to be a challenge. No longer interested in transient whimsy and city life, I was ready to move on from the Chateau. But before I found a new residence, I got a phone call. It was Pat, as usual, with another splendid offer that would surely provide some old-fashioned-high-jinks hilarity.

"Hey, little brother, let's go play this golf course in Palm Springs at the La Quinta Resort. I got us a room for two nights, I'll drive out and pick you up Thursday afternoon, we'll play Friday and Saturday, then I'll drop you off in L.A. Sunday, *on me.*"

Pat had been paying a tout service to pick winners for him in college football games the last few months and his money was well spent. His tout had recently been on a 27–2 run against the spread and Pat had been hammering his hot streak. It always made me happy when Pat hit a hot streak of any kind, because in the grand scheme of things, he had terrible luck compared to me and our brother, Rooster. In 1988, Pat lost his first and only wife, Lori, in a freak car accident, and for twenty-seven years after, he never allowed himself to love or be loved by another female except his dogs Neiman and Mollie.* Like Rooster says, "If it weren't for Pat, we wouldn't understand struggle and we'd have a lot less compassion for people having a hard time." Pat taught us forgiveness. That's why he's my lucky charm.

With the windows down and Boston's "More Than a Feeling" blaring through the speakers, we pulled Pat's dusty and dented Ramcharger dually pickup truck into the La Quinta Resort at eight o'clock that Thursday evening just after sundown. There to greet us in suits and ties were the bellman and manager.

"Good evening, gentlemen, welcome to the La Quinta Hotel and Resort, how was your journey?"

In a headband, sleeveless T-shirt, and a pair of flip-flops, I stepped out of the passenger's door and said, "Great trip, how ya'll doing?," the sound of a large barking dog now echoing through the concourse.

The manager's eyes went to the source of the sound. In the truck bed of Pat's dually was his dog, a very excitable 140-pound black Lab-

---

* Until September 27, 2015, when Emerie James McConaughey was born. Now Pat has a daughter, and someone to love as much as Lori.

rador named Neiman who was aggressively pacing back and forth, impatient to go potty.

"Umm, very well, sir . . . very well," they said.

As I casually crossed to the back of the truck to fetch our luggage and clubs, the manager and bellman kept their distance.

"And may I ask, were you planning on the dog staying with you?" the manager asked.

"Yeah," I said.

"Well, sir . . . we, uh, we don't allow dogs at the resort."

Unloading our golf clubs, without a stutter in my step, I said, "Oh . . . well, this is my brother's Seeing Eye dog."

I made sure to say it loud enough so that Pat, who was now just getting out of the driver's seat, could hear me. As if he'd rehearsed it, Pat raised his left arm up in front of him and appeared to search for the side of the truck, found it, then secured himself to stand up firmly.

"Hang on, Pat, you got it?" I asked.

Pat, eyes half closed in a squint, brought his other hand to the truckside for assurance, "Yeah, buddy, I'm good. We here?"

The manager's chin slightly dropped in embarrassment, then he looked to me with a face that gave me assurance he hadn't put together the implausibility of my *blind brother driving.* My no-flinch Jedi mind trick now successful, I put Neiman on her leash, unloaded her from the truck, and walked her over to Pat.

"Neiman *on,* Pat," I said, to which Pat perfectly enacted a blind man now relaxing because he had his trusty Seeing Eye dog to guide him.

"You good?" I asked.

Pat then did his best Dustin Hoffman in *Rain Man* imitation and said, "Pat good, Neiman on leash," which didn't really make sense to me because he was pretending to be blind, not autistic, but I rolled with it.

The manager and bellhop grabbed and carted our luggage. "Right this way, Mr. McConaughey," they said, and began leading us to our suite. Neiman didn't play her part near as well as my brother and I.

Instead of *leading* Pat, she *pulled* him left and right, pissing on every shrub and Mercedes tire in sight.

"Forty paces straight ahead," I said to Pat, who replied to no one in particular, "Forty paces, yes, forty paces."

The manager and bellman, now very considerate and a bit ashamed at their earlier questioning of the *service* dog, escorted us to our room, where they opened the door, walked the luggage in, and with an excess of civility, made sure Neiman and Pat got into the room safely. Neiman immediately began knocking over furniture, jumping atop the bed, and slobbering on the windows.

"We're here, Pat! This is where we will stay for the next two days!," I said, voice raised for some reason, as if Pat were hard of hearing as well.

"Good, good, this is where we stay!" Pat replied at equal decibel, still squinting and weaving his head left and right like Stevie Wonder.

The manager and the bellman now started backing out of the suite door. "I hope the room is to your liking! We thank you for staying with us!" he said. Now, he was raising *his* voice. "We hope you have a pleasant stay, and if you need *anything,* please let us know!"

"OK, thank you. Pat! Tell the nice men thank you!"

Pat nodded, "Thank you, nice men, thank you," doubling down on his best Raymond Babbitt.

When they shut the door behind them Pat and I fell over laughing. "Thanks a lot, Neiman, you almost blew it for us!"

The next morning, Pat and I were on the tee box for our 8:09 A.M. tee time. I teed off first, then my *blind brother* Pat cranked a three-hundred-yard drive down the middle of the fairway. Pat driving, we hopped into the cart and started to head off for a day on the links when, suddenly, the hotel manager and a security guard hustled up to our side.

Confident he had busted us, but doing his best to remain professional, the manager said, "Good morning, men, uh . . . about the dog?"

He looked at me, and then at Pat. We stared at him as if he had asked a rhetorical question.

"Yeah?" I said.

"I thought you *sa-iiid* he was your *Seeing Eye* dog?"

Oh shit, I thought. *We're busted.*

That's when Pat, cool as can be, without missing a beat, said to the manager almost apologetically, "Oh yeah, I've only got *night* blindness."

The manager's jaw dropped, the security guard leaned back on his heels. We hit the gas and pulled away to play the first of our two rounds of golf that weekend.

After a great weekend of golf, his eyesight now restored, Pat dropped me back at the Chateau.

My trip to Mali had me keen to keep in tune with Mother Nature's rhythm, so I retired my leather pants, boots, and Thunderbird for a pair of board shorts, flip-flops, and a surfboard. It was time to chase the summer at a new address where the Pacific Ocean was my backyard instead of Sunset Boulevard.

I lived on the beach, literally.

I jogged on the beach, I threw Frisbees with Ms. Hud on the beach. I swam in the Pacific, I learned to surf.

I rarely wore a shirt.

I made more films: *How to Lose a Guy in 10 Days, Tiptoes, Sahara, Two for the Money, Failure to Launch,* and *We Are Marshall.*

The romantic comedies remained my only consistent box office hits, which made them my only consistent incoming offers. With their mid-range budgets and the right chemistry between the leads, they were thoroughly successful at the box office. For me personally, I enjoyed being able to give people a ninety-minute breezy romantic getaway from the stress of their lives where they didn't have to think about *anything,* just watch the boy chase the girl, fall down, then get up and finally get her. I had taken the baton from Hugh Grant, and I ran with it.

In the tabloids, the industry, and the public opinion, I became the shirtless, on-the-beach rom-com guy. It became a *thing.* I was also in great shape.

the workout scale

WAKING UP–For some, this is enough.

DRINK A GLASS OF WATER–Hydration for health, that will do it.

TAKING A DEUCE–The morning bowel movement makes your back feel better and your eyes bluer, what else do you need?

WASH DISHES–It's manual labor, that counts.

JUST SCHEDULE IT–You don't have to *actually* work out, just plan on it, that's enough.

MASTURBATION–It's manual labor as well, *and* it cleans the pipes and clears your perspective.

GET A HAIRCUT–More like retail therapy, it makes us feel like we look better, and hence, are in better shape.

PURCHASE A SKINNY MIRROR–Get one like the ones in all the high-end fashion-brand stores. It's an illusion but, hey, when we *look* thinner in the mirror, we *act* thinner in life.

GET A TAN–Like a haircut and a skinny mirror, but it *really* cuts six pounds.

NO MAYO PLEASE–"Cut the mayo, please, I'm on a diet."

NO FRIES WITH THAT–Like the above, this can be a tough duty. "I'll have the Big Mac and a large Coke, but cut the fries, I'm on a diet."

ONE LESS BEER–"I only had eighteen beers today, honey, I usually drink a case. I'm watchin my weight."

STEAM–The nonactive way to generate a sweat from with*out*.

SUBSTITUTE THE FORK WITH CHOPSTICKS–You eat smaller bites of food, which is better for digestion and makes you feel full sooner.

SEX–The original exercise. It generates a sweat from with*in* and improves relationships, making our companion see us in a more flattering light, which psychologically makes us feel like we look better.

BUTT DARTS AND PLYOS—Why go to the gym when you can just take some steroids and do plyometrics on your steering wheel while you drive to and from work?*

BABYSIT THE KIDS—You never sit down, you're always corralling, especially if you have two or more.

TAKE THE STAIRS—No more elevators for you.

DANCE—Probably my favorite one on the list. Cardio, flexibility, and fun. I wish more people were doing more of it.

WALK—Don't ride.

PILATES—Low intensity, excellent for flexibility and core strength.

YOGA—Intense and relaxing. A mental meditation as well.

JOG—Low heart rate but a good fat burner with some distance.

RUN—High intensity, high heart rate.

THE GYM—Our one-stop shop for our entire body, plus it's usually got those skinny mirrors.

A TRAINER—Now you're getting serious. Got someone cracking the whip so you can't procrastinate.

MARATHON—High intensity, long distance, a serious amount of your day spent doing it.

TRIATHLON—Run, bike, swim. For strength, speed, and agility, this is the all-around workout.

Me, I was a daily wake up, take a deuce, get a tan doing yoga on the beach runner who drank a lot of water and danced all night.

How about you?

---

* A friend of mine and chemical engineer, James K., is always jacked up but he never goes to the gym or lifts weights. Instead, he concocts his own juice, injects himself with it, and does plyos on the steering wheel while driving to and from work daily. He told me, "That's why I live thirty miles from my office, make sure I get a good workout."

I was never too bothered by the consistent critical write-offs of me and my work. I enjoyed making romantic comedies, and their paychecks rented the houses on the beaches I ran shirtless on. Getting relative with *this* inevitability, no way was this working-class country boy going to be condescending about the opportunities they gave me, no matter how categorized they were.

That said, as much as I was enjoying the self-engineered *ease* of my life, I was becoming *un*easy with a couple of things. One, the romantic comedies stopped presenting a challenge for me. I felt like I could read the script today and play the part tomorrow. Two, I was beginning to feel like an entertainer, not an actor. *And what is wrong with that?* I asked myself. I had good comedic timing, I had branded *affirmative humor* and *delusional optimism,* I had kept as much masculinity in the neutered rom-com male as you could, and I had succeeded in giving the audience what they wanted.

Still, I felt like I was posturing instead of behaving, *playing a part* instead of being more of myself. What started off fifteen summers before as a highly personal creative expression was nourishing my spirit less and less. Acting was feeling like a means to an end that I had no address for, and if *this* was all acting was for me, then I wasn't sure I wanted to act.

I AM GOOD AT WHAT I LOVE, I DON'T LOVE ALL THAT I'M GOOD AT.

I was getting much more inner growth from my travels than from my career. I loved sales, education, music, and sports. I considered changing professions, maybe start writing short stories and travelogues, going into advertising, or becoming a teacher, a musician, or a football coach. I didn't know.

the grifter

called yurself an
artist

I call yu a grifter

if yu were Picasso

yu coulda stole
from me

but yu showed yur
hand

and yu didn't know
it

a bullshitter
woulda got away
with it

but a liar like yu
can't

my dog coulda
sniffed your royal
scam

yur sleight of hand
ain't too slight
boy

yu thought you'd
meditate me to
sleep but when yu
pulled the trigger
yu wet yourself

cus yu never cocked
yur gun.

Restless again, I needed some evolution. I needed to head *up*river, change lanes, feel some ascension in my grade. But how? Once more, I changed addresses. I bought a house in the Hollywood Hills with a yard big enough to get my hands back in the soil and enough bedrooms for a family of five.

TURN THE PAGE

The late and great University of Texas football coach Darrell Royal was a friend of mine and a good friend to many. A lot of people looked up to him. One was a musician, whom I'll call Larry. Larry was in the prime of his country music career, had number one hits, and his life was rolling. He had picked up a habit snorting "the white stuff" somewhere along the line and at one particular party after a *bathroom break*, Larry strode up to his mentor Darrell and started telling Coach a story. Coach listened, as always, and when Larry finished his story and was about to walk away, Coach Royal put a gentle hand on his shoulder and discreetly said, "Larry, you got something on your nose there, bud." Larry immediately hurried to the bathroom mirror where he saw some white powder he hadn't cleaned off. He was ashamed, embarrassed. Partly because he felt so disrespectful to Coach Royal, but mainly because he'd obviously gotten too comfortable with the drug to even hide it as well as he should.

Well, the next day Larry went to Coach's house and rang the doorbell. Coach answered and Larry said, "Coach, I need to talk to you." Darrell welcomed him in.

Larry confessed. He purged his sins to Coach. He told him how embarrassed he was, and how he'd *lost his way* in the midst of all the fame and fortune. Toward the end of an hour, Larry, now in tears, asked Coach, "What do you think I should do?"

Now, Coach, being a man of few words, said simply, "Larry, **I have never had any trouble turning the page in the book of my life.**" Larry got sober that day and he has been for the last forty-six years.

GREAT LEADERS ARE NOT ALWAYS IN FRONT.

THEY ALSO KNOW WHO TO FOLLOW.

You ever get in a rut? Stuck on the merry-go-round of a bad habit? I have. We are going to make mistakes—own them, make amends, and move on. Guilt and regret kill many a man before their time. Get off the ride. You are the author of the book of your life. Turn the page.

THE ARROW
DOESN'T SEEK
THE TARGET, THE
TARGET DRAWS
THE ARROW

I HAD MET, SPENT TIME with, and seriously dated some wonderful women in my life, many of whom I am still friends with today, but ultimately they were all stops, no stays. In my midthirties, I was looking for a lifetime lover, a best friend, and a mother to be. I was looking for more, I was looking for *the one,* I was looking for *her.*

Then I had another dream. Yes, a wet one.

No, not *that* wet dream, a new one.

Again, I was at peace, this time sitting on the front porch of my one-story, wood-paneled country home in a rocking chair. There was a curbless, horseshoe-shaped dirt driveway that rounded at the three front steps to the elevated ramada I was swaying on. The two-acre green St. Augustine lawn was healthy and uncut. Through the trees in the distance, near the driveway's entrance, Suburbans, Range Rovers, Navigators, and station wagons began to approach the house in a ceremonial procession. Behind the wheel of each automobile was a woman, in the back of each were four young children, all excitedly waving to me as they parked, two tires in the St. Augustine, two on the dirt. Each

223

woman was serene and satisfied. Every child was smiling, laughing, and healthy. We all knew one another very well.

Twenty-two vehicles.

Twenty-two women.

Eighty-eight children.

The women were not there to see a man they had ever married, they were there to see a man they loved and the father of their children. The children were there to see their dad.

Me.

All there to celebrate my eighty-eighth birthday, one child for each year of my life.

Everyone was filled with joy, eager to commemorate my birth, and to see one another. Each mother and I shared an idyllic memory, the children roosted upon my lap. We hugged, we kissed, we laughed and joked, we cried tears of happiness. They all gathered around me on the porch for a family photograph, and we looked toward a large-format box camera on a tripod at the top of the driveway. *Three! Two! One!*

Then I came.

In that dream, I had never married. I was an eighty-eight-year-old bachelor. And *that* notion, for all of my life at that point, would have been a nightmare.

But not in this dream. No, this was a beautiful dream. This dream told me it was okay. It told me *I* was okay.

This dream reminded me that *all I ever knew I wanted to be in life was a father.* The dream also let me know that if I never met *the one* for me and got married, *that* was okay too.

I could have children.

I could become a father.

I could become an eighty-eight-year-old bachelor, surrounded by twenty-two smiling mothers and eighty-eight happy, waving, healthy, and excited children—all of whom I loved, all of whom loved me.

The red light vision of being a lifelong bachelor had come to me in a greenlight wet dream. It was a spiritual sign, a message to surrender, to quit *trying* so intentionally to find the perfect woman for me, and rather, concede to the natural selection process of finding her, her finding me, or not.

So I quit looking for *her.*

Then, she came.

the arrow doesn't seek the target,
the target draws the arrow

We must be aware of what we attract
in life because it is no accident or
coincidence.

The spider waits in his web for
dinner to come.

Yes, we must chase what we want, seek
it out, cast our lines in the water,

but sometimes we don't need to *make*
things happen.

Our souls are infinitely magnetic.

It was July 2005 and I was holding court at the head of the table at the Hyde Club on Sunset Boulevard, handmaking the best margaritas on the planet when I saw her.

A thin, soft, silk turquoise dress draped over caramel-colored shoulders floating right to left across the hazy, low-lit neon room.

She wasn't *delivering* anything.

She wasn't *leaving* anywhere.

She was defying gravity in the direction she wanted to go, and I wanted to be where she was headed. Her head had no bob. Were her

225

feet even *touching* the ground? I couldn't be sure. Like I said, the room was low lit and hazy.

She made an impression *and* a definition:

Naughty and fundamental.

Young with a past.

Homegrown and worldly.

Innocent and cunning.

Springtime and salty.

A squaw and a queen.

She was no virgin but she wasn't for rent.

A mother to be.

She wasn't selling *nothing*. Didn't need to. She knew *what* she was, *who* she was, and she owned it. Her own element. A natural law. A proper noun. Inevitable.

What . . . is . . . that? I said to myself as I rose from my seat, her gravity pulling me. I locked in as she settled on a red velvet chaise longue next to two other women. Unable to catch her eye, I raised my right arm and began to wave, trying to get her attention, when I heard a voice in my left ear.

This is not the type of woman you wave over from across a bar, son. Get your ass up, young man, and go introduce yourself. It was my mom's voice. Time to get relative.

I walked over to the long chair where this woman was midconversation. She looked up.

"Hi, I'm Matthew," I said, as I extended my hand for an honorable shake.

I could tell she recognized me but she remained seated, again, not for sale or easily impressed.

"Camila," she replied as she extended her right arm up and gave an assured yet casual handshake.

I caught my breath.

"Would you . . . and your two friends like to come over to our table? I'll make you a great margarita."

She glanced at her friends.

"Excuse me," she said, then stood up alone and let me escort her over. Even though she left her friends, I could immediately tell that there was no chance she would have come to the table unless I had done the gentlemanly thing and invited them over as well.

I mixed the best margarita I've ever made. I spoke Spanish better than I'd ever spoken it before.

She spoke Portuguese. I've never understood Portuguese as well as I did that night, and haven't since.

The rhythms of the Latin languages seemed to fit the meter. Twenty minutes had passed as we huddled mouth to ear at the end of the table, having our first conversation when—

"McConaughey! Car's out front, let's roll!" my buddy screamed over the music. It was closing time, 2:00 A.M.

"Gimme five minutes!" I said, holding an open palm in front of his face without averting my gaze from hers.

"You wanna come back to my house for a drink?" I asked her. "Me and the boys are going there for a nightcap."

"No, no thanks, not tonight, thanks though," she kindly said.

Shit.

I walked her to her car, which, to her surprise, was not where she had parked it.

"It was right here?!" she said, standing in the vacant parking lot at the gas station next to the club.

"You lookin for a white Aviator?" the gas station attendant who overheard us asked.

"Yes, I am."

"That got towed, this spot is for the gas station only," he said.

"C'mon, one drink at my house," I said. "Then I'll have the chauffeur take you home."

"Okay, sure," she said at last.

We loaded the waiting SUV, my two buddies moved to the third row.

3:30 A.M. My house.

"Well, thanks for the drink, I better go now," she said.

I walked her out to the waiting chauffeur in the driveway, but, for *some* reason, there was no chauffeur waiting in the driveway.

I feigned concern.

"What? Where the heck did he go?" I said. "Unbelievable, I'll call you a cab, sorry."

There was little to no cell service in this part of the Hollywood Hills, but I had a land line so I called three cab companies and guess what? *None* of them either answered or had a driver available.

"You're welcome to take the guest bedroom upstairs."

Now well after four in the morning with *no transportation available,* she acquiesced.

I snuck down to that guest bedroom twice that night to check on her.

I got kicked out both times.

The next morning, I woke up around eleven. As I walked down the spiral staircase to the foyer that led to the kitchen I heard people talking and laughing. The kind of overlapping speech and humor that only people who are extremely comfortable with each other can have. It sounded like old friends.

As I approached the kitchen, there she was, with her back to me, sitting on the center barstool at the cooking area's island, wearing the same turquoise dress over the same caramel shoulders. She was holding court. My housekeeper dished out pancakes to her and my two shirtless friends, who were cackling at the innuendo of a story she'd told less than an hour ago.

It not only *sounded* like old friends, it *looked* like old friends. No juvenile next-morning-walk-of-shame false modesty, no rush to get out of a house she never intended on staying at overnight, no, just good-humored grace and confidence.

I called the gas station where her car was towed and found out where it had been taken. It was an hour's drive to the impoundment lot. I insisted on driving her there. On the way, I put one of my favorite CDs in the slot, a reggae artist named Mishka, whose album I was producing at the time.[*]

I drove. We listened. Two, three songs in a row would play without either of us uttering a word. Neither of us *feeling* like we needed to say a thing. Neither of us anxious to fill the quiet gaps. The silence wasn't awkward, it was golden.

We arrived at the impound, both wishing it were in Florida instead. Before parting I asked for her phone number. She reached into her purse, pulled out a crumpled piece of spiral notebook paper, and wrote it down.

I went in for a kiss goodbye. She turned her head, but not far enough to where I couldn't catch a quarter inch of the left side of her lips.

I asked her if she wanted to go out that evening.

"Yes," she said. "But I can't. It's my dad's birthday tonight."

"What about tomorrow night?"

"Call me."

I waved as I pulled away; she waved back.

That mermaid from the Amazon nine years ago *had* seen me. Then she swam into the deeper waters of the Atlantic, around Cape Horn, and up the Pacific, where she finally disembarked in Hollywood, then came to a club on Sunset Boulevard where I recognized her turquoise shape and caramel shoulders swimming across the room and into my affection.

Fifteen years later she's still the only woman I've ever wanted to take on a date, sleep with, or wake up next to.

GREENLIGHT.

---

[*] I first heard Mishka in Jamaica at the turn of the millennium and instantly loved his music. I found him five years later in the Caribbean and soon we decided to make music together, so I started j.k. livin Records and produced a couple of albums with him.

oh lady of good hope

Oh my love, how are
you?

To see you, not
make you, happy

Is one of my
favorite things to
do

My sister, my
lover, my buddy, my
clone

Headfirst through
these days

We charge alone

And now we're at
that place

Just glancing over
the edge

*"You go first, no
you go."*

What if we held
hands, jumped
together?

What a long way
down it is,

we both agree it's
true.

"Good thing," I
say.

You say, *"What?"*

*"I only wanna fly
with you."*

Camila and I had been dating for about a year when I took a job in Australia on the film *Fool's Gold*. Until then, I had always gone to work alone and lived solitarily on location, but this woman was something, someone, different in my life. I wanted her to come to Australia for the three months I was filming, live with me in the two-bedroom beach house in Port Douglas I'd be renting. I didn't like the idea of being away from her while I was there. I liked the idea of being *with* her while I was. I invited her.

"Are you sure?" she asked.

"Yes, I am."

"Are. You. Sure?"

"Yes, I am."

"Well, there's a few things that I'll need in order to do that. I'll need my own bedroom, my own bathroom, and my own key to the house."

"Deal."

She came. She stayed. She didn't sleep in that bedroom, seldom used that bathroom, and rarely needed that other key. But she still had them, and it was an important part of her independence, of *our* independence, at this stage of our relationship. Very wise real estate to claim, whether you use it or not.

About two months in, with New Year's coming up, I found a six-day surf retreat in Papua New Guinea for the break. Tree houses, jungle, surf, adventure.

We spent our days surfing, swimming, diving, hiking the rain forest, exploring the markets, and visiting indigenous tribes. We lived in a one-room tree house on the edge of the jungle, no electricity, none needed. It was wild, beautiful, magical.

On the fourth afternoon, after making love, we were sitting on the porch perch of our tree hut, watching the sun set over the Solomon Sea, having our first cocktail before joining the locals at a watering hole a few hundred yards down the beach.

I was falling in love.

"What would I have to do to lose you?" I asked.

As I said these words I turned to look at her out of the corner of my eyes, the drink in her right hand already halfway to her mouth as she was moving to take a sip of it. How graceful her hand moved, never hitching, never hesitating, just fluently gliding as it would have if a question like that had never been asked.

The drink reached her lips, and she took a nice, easy sip, her eyes staying with the sunset. Then, she took a relaxed, satisfied swallow, and slowly lowered the glass back down to its wet ring resting place on the wooden arm of her chair.

"Oh, that's easy," she said as she turned her head to me. My heart raced. Her eyes found mine and settled. "Change," she said.

When we returned from Australia, Camila moved west from New York. My Hollywood Hills home was an ideal nest for two serious lovers but it was *mine,* and without saying it, we both knew we wanted a fresh start, an opportunity to build a life together. The two of us relocated to the Malibu Beach RV park, where we moved into my twenty-eight-foot Airstream, "the Canoe." Dedicated to a future with each other, we discussed children, and soon decided she would get off birth control.

"On one condition," she said. "When you go off to work, we *all* go."*

---

* For the past twelve years, Camila and all of our children have always traveled and lived with me on every location my acting career ever took me.

today I made love to my woman.

Not because I wanted to right then,

but because I knew I'd want to once we
started.

And that the walk on the beach we took
afterward would be more romantic.

The cocktail I made at 5:45 would taste
better.

The shrimp I seasoned would have more
savor.

The All-Star game we watched at 7 would be
more exciting.

The music we danced to till midnight would
have more rhythm.

And the conversation about life we had
together sitting across the kitchen table
from each other until 3 in the morning
would be more inspiring . . .

And it was.

"Deal," I said.

For months we covered all 188 square feet of "the Canoe" trying, but nothing stuck, so we forgot about *trying* and just enjoyed the *doing*.

A few months later I got home around seven one night and she was there to greet me with her usual hug, kiss, and a smile. The kiss was a little wetter this evening.

She handed me a prepoured double tequila on the rocks. I kicked off my flip-flops and sat down on the couch. One of my favorite scents was coming from the stove top: homemade cheeseburgers.

"What's up? This is heaven on earth."

233

"Yes, it is," she said, as she sat down next to me and handed me a small wooden box wrapped in a string of turquoise stones.

I opened it. Inside was a photograph. I couldn't quite make out what it was so I had a closer look to see more clearly.

Tears of joy began to run down my cheeks. I looked her way. She was crying the same tears. The photograph was an ultrasound. She was pregnant.

We cried, we laughed, we danced.

The only thing I ever knew I wanted to be was a father.

To me, *fatherhood* meant a man had *made it* in life. Growing up, I said "yes sir" and "no sir" to my father and his friends *because* they were fathers. Fatherhood, what I most revered in life, what I was **most impressed** with, was now what I was about to become **more involved** with. The message of manhood that came to me at my own father's passing had newborn relevance as I became one myself.

Yes sir.

GREENLIGHT.

Around 10:00 P.M., we called my mom to share the news. It was midnight Texas time.

"Mom? Me and Camila here. We have some great news we wanna share with you, you're on speakerphone."

"Oh great, I love good news. Hi, Camila!"

"Hi, Mrs. McConaughey!"

"Mom?"

"Yeah."

"Camila and I made a baby. She's pregnant."

Silence.

More silence.

"Mom? . . . You there?"

"No! . . . No! No! Nooooooo! Matthew!!! This is *out* of *order*! No, no, no, no, noooooo! Matthew! I raised you to get married *before* you had a baby! With anyone! *No*!!! This is *all* wrong, oh no, Matthew, this is *not* good news."

Camila and I looked at each other, our mouths agape. I reached toward the phone, tempted to take it off speaker and spare Camila the drubbing. Then I thought, no, best she gets to know every bit of my mom.

"Oh geez, Mom. I thought you'd be so happy. Me and Camila are overjoyed."

"Well, I'm *not*!! . . . This is all wrong, Matthew. This is *not* how I raised you, and I'm sorry, Camila, but this is *not* how I raised my son. I am *not* happy in the least," she said.

Then she hung up.

Camila and I absorbed the blow, our tears of joy dried up with shock.

"Oh shit," Camila said.

"*No* shit," I replied.

We leaned back on the couch, catching our breath.

Camila poured me another drink. I didn't take a sip, I took a swig.

A few minutes later my phone rang. It was Mom. *What were we in for now?* I answered.

"Mom?"

"Yeah, am I on speakerphone? Camila, can you hear me?"

"Yes, Mrs. McConaughey, I'm here."

"What's up, Mom?"

"Well . . . I'd like to put some *Wite-Out* over that last conversation. I realize I was being selfish. I don't have to agree with the *order* of events, but it's not my right to judge them. As long as *you're* happy, then *I'm* happy for you . . . Okay?"

I stared at the phone and shook my head.

"*Wite-Out* it is, Mrs. McConaughey!" Camila said, stifling her laughter.

"Great, cus everybody deserves a do-over! Love you, bye."

And with that, she hung up.

IMPRESSIONS

We've all encountered
those people, who, out of
the corner of our eye,
from across the street,
at magic hour, appear
astoundingly attractive,
even God- or Goddess-like.
The way they move, the
way the light hits them,
invokes reverence and awe.
The IMPRESSION.

And then we got a closer
look. Damnit. Letdown.
Good from afar, but far
from good.

Some people will never be
more attractive than in
that first impression,
from a distance, in that
light, at that time, in
that way we saw them, when
our hopes became highest
and our wish fulfillment
was fully leaded. They
will never look better
than in that initial,
fuzzy-edged glimpse. The
impression. The WIDE SHOT.

Some relationships are
better in a wide shot.
More impressive in the
impression.

Like in-laws. Best to only
see on holidays.

Like neighbors. It's why
we have walls and fences.

Like that long-distance
romance that fell apart
when you moved in
together.

Like that summer fling
that only lasted through
August.

That friend that became a
lover that you now miss as
a friend.

Like ourselves when we're
a fraud.

They're better from
a distance. With less
frequency. With less
intimacy.

Sometimes we need more
space.

It's romance, it's
imagination.

Distance is the flirt and
the wink, it's frivolous,
it's mysterious, a
fantasy. A constant
honeymoon because we can't
quite see it, we aren't
quite sure about it, we
don't quite know it.

It's a fuck. It's
detachment. It's separate.
It's public. It's
carefree. It's painless.
It's for rent.

And we like it that way,
because sometimes it's
better with the lights
dimmed.

The MIRROR

We've all encountered those people, who, when we look them in the eye, when they're right in front of us, in broad daylight, appear astoundingly attractive, even God- or Goddess-like. The way they move, the way the light hits them, invokes reverence and awe. The DEFINITION.

And then the closer we look. Wow. We take flight. Good from close, better close-up.

Some people get more attractive, have a greater impression on us the more we see them, the closer we look, in that light, at that time, in the way we see them, when our hopes are highest and our wish fulfillment is fully leaded. They will always look better the more clearly we see them. The definition. The CLOSE-UP.

Some relationships are better in a close-up. More impressive with more definition.

Like the woman whose photograph doesn't turn you on, but in real life she does.

Like our children.

Like our spouse.

Like a best friend.

Like God.

Like ourselves when we're authentic and true.

They're better up close, with more frequency, with more intimacy.

Sometimes we need to be near.

It's love, it's literal.

Closeness is the quiet moments together, the pain shared, the beauty seen, the honesty. It's authentic. It's reality. A constant relationship because we can see it, we're sure about it, we know it.

It's making love. It's attachment. It's togetherness. It's private. It costs us. It hurts. We own it.

And we like it that way, because sometimes it's better with the lights on.

Impressions in the Mirror

Camila was six months pregnant when I got a call from my film production office in Venice, California. The number came up on caller ID and I reached to pick up the phone.

My hand *paused* midreach.

I didn't want to answer it. A call from *my* production office. The office where *I* had paid the rent and staff since 1996.

I didn't answer it. Instead, I called my lawyer, Kevin Morris.

"I'm shutting down the production company immediately. I'll call everybody and let em know tomorrow. I want to give generous severance packages. Shut down j.k. livin Records as well."

It was time to clean house. *Process of elimination.*

I had five things on my proverbial desk to tend to daily: family, foundation, acting, a production company, and a music label. I felt like I was making B's in all five. By shutting down the production company and the music label, I eliminated two of my five commitments with plans to make A's in the other three.

I told my lawyer that I wanted to take care of my family, my foundation, and be an actor for hire.

Simplify, focus, conserve to liberate.

Alright, alright, alright.

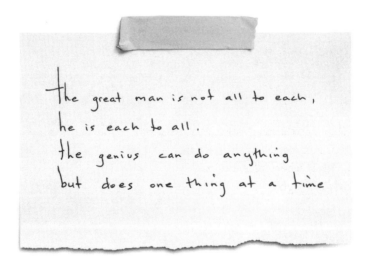

the great man is not all to each,
he is each to all.
the genius can do anything
but does one thing at a time

On July 7, 2008, after three days of labor and an emergency C-section, Camila gave birth to a seven-pound, eight-ounce baby boy.

We didn't know the gender beforehand, which is one of the best surprises you can ever give yourself. We were set for a name if it was a baby girl, but we had a pretty long and interesting list if it was a boy.

"Matthew." "Man." "Medley." "Igloo." "Mister." "Citizen." "Levi."

You know, the usuals.

Camila preferred "Matthew." Me, I was concerned about the *Jr.* aspect and *the same name as the famous dad snare,* but right now, we weren't thinking about names, we were too busy smiling, laughing, crying, and loving.

About an hour and a half after the birth, a nurse came in and handed me a formal document to fill out. It read:

On July 7, 2008, at **6:22** pm,

_____ was born.

(name)

6:22. My favorite Bible verse:

If thine eye be single,
Thy whole body will be full of light.

—MATTHEW 6:22

The mandorla.
The paradox instead of the contradiction.
The union instead of the friction.
The place where *all* the colors live.
The white light.

The third eye.

A verse that has given me spiritual guidance for decades, **6:22** was even carved into Camila's and my bedroom door by two Dogon tribesmen I commissioned in Mali back in 2000.

The apostle "Matthew" was also known as "Levi" in other parts of the world. Same man. Different name.

From Leviticus, the third book in the bible of law and ritual.

Levitical. Levitated. Levi. **Matthew 6:22.**

So, on July 7, 2008, at 6:22 P.M., **Levi** Alves McConaughey was born. His middle name, Alves, is Camila's maiden name.

GREENLIGHT.

```
Man is never more masculine than after
the birth of his first child. Not macho.
Masculine. After his firstborn, a new
father's head, heart, and gut are more
aligned than they have ever been. His
five senses on the same frequency, his
intuition is in tune, he should engrave
any instinct he has for the next six
months-personal, financial, spiritual,
or career. He should trust that he
kn-owwws and kn-owww that he can tell
the future, because now, for the first
time in his life, he is livin for it and
it is livin for him.

Bet it all and sweep the board.
```

Just as I was introduced to new life, a possibly fatal family crisis unexpectedly hit at home and I rushed back to Austin to be with my mom and brothers. Camila and Levi joined me after a couple of weeks and we rented a small home in my mom's active retirement community where we slept on blow-up air mattresses.

I don't know about *all* retirement communities but *this* one was cool. A bunch of old people minding to themselves, not looking for anything or anyone else to give them significance for *anything*. It's like they got into older age and became revolutionaries again, or anarchists. They were like kids.

They're God-loving patriotic Americans with wild senses of humor and a total lack of pretense or political correctness. They laugh at *everything,* and love getting laughed *at.* They also love to have a good chat and offer unsolicited life advice.

*"You always look like you're havin fun
when I see your work, Matthew, and that's
what life's all about, keep havin fun."*

*"The greatest achievement in life is your
kids, Matthew, so have a bunch, and
remember, grandkids are twice as nice and
half the work."*

Being surrounded by senior citizens will remind you of your mortality and make you feel younger at the same time. You see their bodies not doing what their minds tell them to do and their minds forgetting what they know to remember, yet they're anything but sentimental about it. They get a routine and stick to it: going to the gym, stopping by for an evening cocktail, singing in the church choir, and signing up for every activity offered.

*"Staying active and social, Matthew,
that's the key to longevity."*

On our way back to the rental house after an early-evening bingo match at the recreation center, Camila and I were stopped at a red light.

"You wanna move back to Texas, don't you?" she unexpectedly asked.

I *had* been thinking about it. Maybe it was the manners, the value people put on common sense, the fact that when you're playing baseball in the front yard and a car stops to have a look, it's a well-wishing neighbor instead of paparazzi. Maybe it was the optimism and the fact that nobody acts like there's a crisis even when there is one. Maybe it was that Mom was now in her late seventies and by football math that was at least the fourth quarter and seeing her more than twice a year seemed a prudent proposition. The answer was that

Camila and I had just started a family and I wanted our children to have all of the above.

I turned to meet her gaze.

"Yep."

She took a deep breath, nodded her head left to right with a shrewd grin. "You son of a bitch." Then she gave a glance to baby Levi in the car seat behind us.

"Let's do it."

The light turned green. I hit the gas.

LIFE. LIKE ARCHITECTURE. IS A VERB.
IF DESIGNED WELL. IT WORKS. IT'S BEAUTIFUL. AND
IT NEEDS NO DIRECTIONS. IT NEEDS MAINTENANCE.

After taking care of the family dilemma that brought me back to Texas, Camila, Levi, and I bought and moved into a home on the outskirts of Austin, overlooking the river.

Nine acres, a spring-fed well, and a deed for a plot of land at the water's edge for a boathouse that the seller forgot to list as a feature. More than enough room to have some dogs, raise a family, and bang on my congas in my birthday suit without disturbing a neighbor.

Just as the early death of my father made me level up and become a man, the family emergency along with fatherhood helped me more deeply reconsider my life and who I was in it. Especially with my career. Death, family crisis, and newborns—the end of a life, trying to keep a life, and welcoming in a new one—these are three things that will shake your floor, give you clarity, remind you of your mortality, and hence, give you courage to live harder, stronger, and truer. Three things that make you ask yourself,

"What matters?"
Three things that make you realize,
"It *all* does."

```
In the fact of fate that death
and birth bring

we recognize we are both human
and God.

We find the belief that our
choices matter,

that it's not all for nothing,

it's all for everything
```

I was a successful actor, a celebrity, and a movie star. I didn't have to worry about putting food on the table or paying rent, but my career path and the characters and films I was getting offered and doing were not satisfying me anymore. Bored with the rom-com roles and the worlds they inhabited, I'd been going to bed with an itchy butt, waking up with a stinky finger for long enough.

My life was full. Wild. Dangerous. Essential. Consequential. Lively. I laughed louder, cried harder, loved bigger, loathed deeper, and felt *more* as the man in my life than in the characters I was playing in the movies. I appreciated the fact that if it had to be imbalanced one way or the other, a vital existence was more important than a vital profession, but I wanted to be in stories that at least challenged the vibrancy of the life I was livin, and play characters that at least challenged the liveliness of the man I was.

Those roles and stories I was looking for? The ones that would compete with the life I was livin? They weren't coming my way, and again, I wasn't sleeping well with the ones that were. It was time to make a change, to pivot, to make a new commitment. No more changing addresses hoping the weather would change. This time, with more than ever to live *for,* it was time to quit leaving crumbs, time to get truly selfish, and see what I could live without.

It was time for real sacrifice. Plus, Camila was pregnant again.

IT'S NOT A RISK UNLESS YOU CAN LOSE THE FIGHT

BE BRAVE,
TAKE THE HILL

WHEN FACING ANY CRISIS, FROM Hurricane Katrina to a family emergency, to the profound choices we have to make in life, I've found that a good plan is to first **recognize** the problem, then **stabilize** the situation, **organize** the response, then **respond**. Aware that I needed *more* as an actor, I'd recognized the problem. Now it was time to pivot and stabilize my situation.

I called my money manager, Blaine Lourd, and asked how long I could go without working and still live the life we were accustomed to.

"You saved your money well, do what you need to do," he said.

I called my agent, Jim Toth, and told him that I wanted to stop doing romantic comedies to find dramatic work that challenged me.

"No problem," he quickly replied.

"What do you mean, 'No problem'?" I asked. "My rom-coms have been bringing in a healthy 10 percent commission to your agency's wallet for over a decade. What do you think your bosses are gonna say when you go in the Monday morning meeting and tell them, 'McConaughey's not doing romantic comedies anymore'!?"

"I don't work for them, Mr. McConaughey, I work for you."
Mensch.

selfish

When I'm rich
enough to not care
about the money.

When a child's
life is more
important than my
own.

When my self-worth
isn't reliant on
the adulation of
others.

When I don't
care anymore,
to outscore my
desires,

I look near and
within, and get
self-ish.

This is the
measure of a man's
greatness,

when a man becomes
classic.

When mortal
rewards are no
longer enough to
pay his rent,

man becomes
legend.

Fish for yourself.

Self-ish.

It was a risky bet I was making. In Hollywood, if you pass on *too many* projects, they may quit asking. If you step out of your lane, and turn your back on what you're successful at, the industry can turn its back on you. They don't mind seeing you miss the bus because there's plenty of people to take your seat. Again, it's not personal, it's just business.

I wet the floor with my tears talking to Camila about this decision. We cried. We prayed. We made a deal.

"It's gonna be dry weather for a while, honey," she said. "Who knows how long it will last. It's going to be hard. I know you're gonna get antsy, I know you're gonna get wobbly, I know you're gonna drink more, but . . . If we're gonna do this, if we're gonna *commit* to this change, then we're gonna do it all the way. No half-assin it. Deal?"

Just like my dad told me years ago.

"Deal."

At a crossroads not a catastrophe, I knew my existential dilemma was going to cost me, monetarily sure, but even more so emotionally. The fatigue of not knowing if and when I would come out of it was going to be a test. By telling *Hollywood,* my mistress of the last almost twenty years, *I still love you, but we need a break, and I'd rather be alone and happy than together and not,* I was now in limbo. I'd purchased a one-way ticket to *will notify.* I prepared for the worst and hoped for the best.

The holidays were coming up and I was looking forward to spending time with my family. The more family I could be around, the less I would think about the career I was walking away from, and the more I would be reminded of where I came from.

Each Christmas we all go to my brother's ranch in West Texas for our yearly reunion. Everyone loads up their trucks and RVs with their kids and dogs and heads to the ranch, where we catch up with each other, drink, eat, and tell lies. During the days we hike the rugged West Texas terrain, deer hunt, ride horses, feed cows, watch bowl games on TV, and then end up around a campfire at night telling new stories and resurrecting old ones until deep into the morning. As religious as we were raised, these family gatherings now offered very little Christmas ritual besides opening presents on the twenty-fifth. No family

sit-down dinner, no Bible readings, just all of us together for a five-day 24-7 onslaught of beef, bullshit, no curfews, optional showering, and drinking to remember, not to forget.

If anyone ever shows up on their *high horse* or is *walkin on their toes,* as Mom calls it, the rest of the family will rip them back down to earth until they cry for mercy, then we lift them back up off the ground and serve them a drink. There are always a few tears shed but a hundred percent forgiveness by the time we leave, because, as my brother Rooster says, "If everything we did was right, we'd never know what was wrong."

I'd been on the receiving end of a few of these humble pie interventions but not this year; no, my family knew I was going through a challenging time. If anything, they were wondering *just what in the hell was wrong with me* turning down regular work and hefty paychecks, but they could tell my mind was made up, and my family always respected sincere conviction, which I now had.

A couple days after Christmas, Rooster, Pat, and I were riding around the ranch sipping beers in Pat's maroon dually truck when Pat, who was then and still is a pipe salesman working *for* Rooster, decided to call into his answering service to see what business-related messages he might have missed over the Christmas break. Pat had one of those 24-7 virtual receptionist services where you call in with your ID number and they relay your missed messages. He dialed the 1-800 digits.

"This is 812," he says.

"Yes, 812, give me just a moment . . ."

Ten seconds pass.

"Um, sir. That account appears to *not* be active."

"What do you mean '*not active*'?"

"I mean it is *out of service,* sir."

"But that's the ID you gave me to call in and check my messages."

"I understand that, sir, but account 812 has, it says here, been *inactive* for over . . . *two years.*"

GREENLIGHTS

Pat, beginning to fume, immediately slammed the brakes, hopped out of the truck, and started yelling at the other end of the line,

"What do you mean it's been down for over two years! Do you know how many millions of dollars that I lost from business calls coming in, to me, to buy pipe, from me, and they couldn't even leave a message, for me, because *you* had my account inactive!!! I am gonna sue your ass! I'm taking you to court! *Two years* my account's been down and it's *your* fault!"

"Uh . . . sir, I'm just the person who answers the phone and connects people with their accounts, and yours, sir, is *not* active."

"I don't give a damn what you say, I've probably lost at least ten million dollars *because* you haven't been takin my messages in over two years! Ten million dollars, lady! That's what I'm suing you for!"

She hung up on him. Pat continued his rant.

"Don't you dare hang up on me, you hear me! You OWE me!"

Finally closing his flip phone, Pat kicked the dirt, then turned to me and Rooster who had been witnessing the tirade.

"You believe that shit?! Two years they've had my account inactive, two fuckin years! I'm suing those fuckers for ten million! I'll take this all the way to the Supreme Court if I have to!"

That's when Rooster asked Pat a question he obviously had not considered.

"Well, little brother, what do you think the judge is gonna say in court when he finds out that you didn't even *know* it was down 'cause you hadn't even called in to check your messages in over *two* years?"

Case closed.

I guess everybody in my family has a passion for prosecution, we just have trouble picking litigations we can win.

IF WE ALL MADE SENSE OF HUMOR THE DEFAULT EMOTION. WE'D ALL GET ALONG BETTER.

The next day, Camila, Levi, and I had to cut the holiday soirée short and head back home to take care of a more time-sensitive affair.

I believe trying to maintain a honeymoon glow in a relationship is a fool's errand fantasy. Worse yet, it's unfair to the two lovers trying to maintain it. It's a 120-watt bulb that burns too hot to last. No one can live up to the pedestal we put them on if we always put them *on* one. As well, when we only see our lover as a superhuman, our reflection in their eyes makes us one to them in theirs. Then we're both for rent, because we're both unobtainable.

The honeymoon, like *Hollywood,* is an animated movie. It's larger than life, not a reality we should expect to see once we exit the theater.

Where we live. Where our humanity lives. Where our secrets, scars, fears, hopes, and failures reside. This is what comes after the credits roll. Where real love cares, hurts, understands, falls down, and gets back up. Where it's not easy, but we get to honestly try.

The twenty-watt bulb isn't enough light to show the way if I expect *you* to be Wonder Woman and you only see *me* as Mr. Incredible.

The hundred-watt honeymoon bulb *is* superhuman.

By design.

It's the beginning, the first time, the birth. That's why it's called a honeymoon, not a marriage. It's not obtainable, or sustainable.

Until you have a daughter.

On January 3, 2010, Vida Alves McConaughey was born.

The only honeymoon that lasts forever.

GREENLIGHT.

define success
for yourself

I went to a voodoo shop south of New Orleans the
other day. It had vials of "magic" potions stacked
in columns with labels defining what they would give
you: Fertility, Health, Family, Legal Help, Energy,
Forgiveness, Money.

Guess which column was sold out? Money. Yep, money is
king currency today. Money is success. The more we have,
the more successful we are, right?

Even our cultural values have been financialized.
Humility is not in vogue anymore, it's too passive. We
can get rich quick on an Internet scam, be an expert at
nothing but everything if we say we are, get famous for
our sex tape, and attain wealth, fame, rank, and power,
even respect, without having a shred of competence for
anything of value. It happens every day.

We all want to succeed. The question we need to ask
ourselves is, What is success to us? More money? Okay.
A healthy family? A happy marriage? Helping others? To
be famous? Spiritually sound? To express ourselves? To
create art? To leave the world a better place than we
found it?

"What is success to me?" Continue to ask yourself
that question. How are *you* prosperous? What is *your*
relevance? Your answer may change over time and that's
fine, but do yourself this favor: Whatever your answer
is, don't choose anything that will jeopardize your
soul. Prioritize who you are, who you want to be, and
don't spend time with anything that antagonizes your
character. Don't depend on drinking the Kool-Aid.
It's popular, tastes sweet today, but it will give you
cavities tomorrow.

Life is not a popularity contest. Be brave, take the
hill, but first, answer the question, "What is my hill?"

A YEAR WENT BY.

Dozens of romantic comedy offers came my way. *Only* romantic comedy offers came my way. I read them out of respect but I stayed the course, stuck to the plan, and ultimately passed on them all. Just *how* puritanical was I about it?

Well, I got a $5 million offer for two months' work on one. I read it. I passed.

Then they offered $8 million. Nope.

They then offered $10 million. No, thank you.

Then $12.5 million. Not this time, but . . . thanks.

Then $14.5 million.

Hmmmm . . . Let me reread it.

And you know what? It was a *better* script. It was funnier, more dramatic, just an overall *higher quality* script than the first one I read with the $5 million offer. It was the same script, with the exact same words in it, but it was far superior to the previous ones.

I declined the offer.

If I couldn't do what I wanted, I wasn't going to do what I didn't, no matter the price.

TRUTH'S LIKE A JALAPEÑO, THE CLOSER TO THE ROOT THE HOTTER IT GETS.

A sense of humor helped me cope, a strong woman by my side kept me steadfast, and an infant son and newborn daughter to raise kept me busy. Together, they all helped me navigate my self-induced hiatus from Hollywood. I continually had to reinforce my belief that my holdout was a form of delayed gratification, that today's abstinence was an investment that would give me ROI tomorrow, that my personal protest was going to mail residuals to my soul down the road, that I was, as Warren Buffett says, buying straw hats in the winter. But being out of the limelight, *not working, was* taking its toll.

I've always needed work for my own sense of self-significance. For eighteen years, I'd had the honor of being addicted to acting and making movies, and now, without it, my dependency on it was causing a good amount of anxiety. With each rom-com offer that came in I couldn't help but think about the opportunity to work again, on anything. My need for immediate personal accomplishment had me fighting against the temptation to do what I had always felt privileged to be able to do in the first place, while fighting *for* the necessity to have my art, my work, more resemble myself and my life.

TEN MORE MONTHS WENT BY.

It was evident that the industry, the studio heads, the producers, the directors, the casting agents, all of them, *had* gotten my message because now *nothing* came in. No rom-coms, nada. Not one single offer. For *anything*.

A total of twenty months had passed where I said no to anything that had defined my brand before:

Rom-com guy. No.

Shirtless-on-the-beach guy. Nope, no beaches or paparazzi in Austin.

For twenty months I did not give the public or the industry any more of what they had banked on me to give them. No more of what they expected and even assumed to know. For twenty months I removed myself from the public eye. At home in Texas with Camila, I was raising Levi and Vida, gardening, writing, praying, visiting old friends, spending time with family, and recoiling from relapse. The industry didn't know *where* I was, just what I wasn't doing. Out of sight, I was out of mind. It seemed I *was* forgotten.

voluntary obligations

Moms and dads teach us things as children.
Teachers, mentors, the government, and
laws all give us guidelines to navigate
life, rules to abide by in the name of
accountability and order.

I'm not talking about those obligations.
I'm talking about the ones we make with
ourselves. The YOU versus YOU obligations.
Not the societal regulations and
expectations that we acknowledge and endow
for anyone other than ourselves, these
are faith-based responsibilities that we
make on our own, the ones that define our
constitution and character.

They are secrets with our self, personal
protocols, private counsel in the court of
our own conscience, and while nobody will
give us a medal or throw us a party when
we abide by them, no one will apprehend us
when we don't, because no one will know,
except us.

An honest man's pillow is his peace of
mind, and when we lie down on ours at
night, no matter who's in our bed, we *all*
sleep alone. The voluntary obligations are
our personal Jiminy Crickets, and there
are not enough cops in the entire world to
police them—it's on us.

Then, after just shy of two years of being gone from the industry
and sending a very deliberate message to Hollywood as to what I was
not anymore, I suddenly and unexpectedly became something, a *new
good idea.*

The anonymity and unfamiliarity had bred creativity. Casting Matthew McConaughey as the defense attorney in *The Lincoln Lawyer* was now a fresh thought. Going to McConaughey for the lead in *Killer Joe* was now a novel notion.

Richard Linklater called me for *Bernie.*

Lee Daniels came to me for *The Paperboy.*

Jeff Nichols wrote *Mud* for me.

Steven Soderbergh called for *Magic Mike.*

Yes, by saying *no.*

The target drew the arrow.

I was remembered by being forgotten.

I had **un-branded.**

I was a *re*-discovery, and now it was time to *in*vent.

My sacrifice complete, I had weathered the storm.

Organized, I knew what I wanted, and I was ready to respond.

It was time for *me* to say *yes,* and **re-brand.**

Fuck the bucks. I'm going for the experience.

GREENLIGHT.

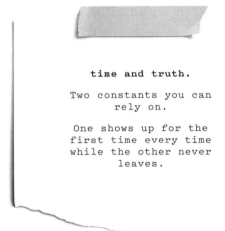

time and truth.

Two constants you can
rely on.

One shows up for the
first time every time
while the other never
leaves.

The offers came in droves, almost as many as after *A Time to Kill.* The difference this time was that I knew what roles and stories I wanted to do and my appetite for dangerous dramatic fare was ravenous. Camila's appetite for her man carving his own path had teeth as well.

At one point I had offers for roles in *The Paperboy, Magic Mike,* and *Mud,* all three of which I dearly wanted to do, but their production schedules were going to be back to back to back if I did all three, leaving me only a few weeks in between each to prepare if I did them all.

I remember saying to Camila, "I think I have to choose two of the three so I have the eight weeks I need to prepare for the two movies I choose to do."

"You *want* to do all three?" she asked.

"Yeah, but the schedule's too tight for me to prepare like I think I need to."

"If you *want* to do all three, then reach between your legs and grab your pair, *big boy,* do all three, you'll make it work."

I did and it did.

I'd read the *Dallas Buyers Club* script in 2007 and immediately attached myself to it as the actor who would play the lead character Ron Woodroof. Once again, I was drawn to a character on the fringes of society, an underdog, an outlaw, doing what was necessary to survive. Being *attached* meant I had control of the script and could try and get it made, as well as approve the director. For the few years before and during my twenty-month sabbatical, no directors or financiers were interested in making a period drama about AIDS with *Rom-Com McConaughey* in the lead. Even early into my re-branding phase, with the so-called *McConaissance** picking up steam, nobody was interested. Plenty of other actors tried to take control of the script away from me, and many other directors wanted to make the film with someone other than me, but I held on to it with a firm hand.

Then, in January 2012, my agent told me a Canadian director named Jean-Marc Vallée had read the script and was interested in meeting me. I watched a film of his, *C.R.A.Z.Y.*, and liked it for all the right reasons. Unsentimental humor and heart with anarchy wrapped around a dreamer's humanity. It also had a badass soundtrack, which I still have no idea how he got on the low budget he had. This was exactly what I felt the *Dallas Buyers Club* script needed to bring it to life. We met in New York and discussed our passion for the project. Having recently done *Magic Mike*, I was in excellent physical shape.

"This character, Ron Woodroof, he has Stage 4 HIV, how are *you* going to look like *you* do?" he asked.

"Because it's my job to and I will," I told him. "It's my responsibility to Ron."

A week later he agreed to direct.

Jean-Marc, the producers Robbie Brenner, Rachel Winter, and I made a plan to make the film in October of that year. Weighing 182 pounds at the time, I had a lot of weight to lose. Five months out from our "agreed upon" start date, I began shedding weight. Three egg whites in the morning, five ounces of fish and a cup of

---

* Did you know I made up, coined, and created the term *McConaissance?* I did.

I was at Sundance with *Mud* in 2013 when I sat down for an interview with MTV. I'd been on a pretty good career run and I figured it needed a campaign slogan, an anthem, a bumpersticker, but I knew it couldn't come from me.

"You've been on quite the run, Mr. McConaughey. *Killer Joe, Bernie, Magic Mike,* now *Mud.* Congratulations," the journalist said.

"Thank you, yeah, I'm on a great ride, I actually did an interview the other day and the journalist called it a 'McConaissance,'" I replied.

"Oh my gosh, the 'McConaissance.' That's brilliant. That may stick." It did.

I've never told anybody that story until now.

steamed vegetables for lunch, the same for dinner, and as much wine as I wanted was my diet. I shed two and a half pounds a week like clockwork.

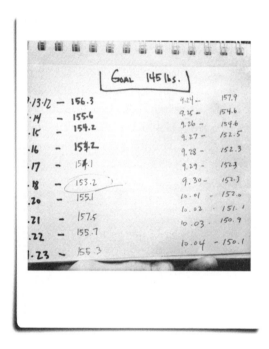

At 157 pounds, with more to lose, I received a call from Martin Scorsese offering me the two-day role of the broker-mentor Mark Hanna to Leonardo DiCaprio's Jordan Belfort in the film *The Wolf of Wall Street*. Remember what I said about those launchpad lines? When I read the script and saw that Mark Hanna's secret to successful stock brokering was *cocaine and hookers,* I took flight. Delusional or not, anyone who believes *that* could have an encyclopedia written about him. So I started writing it. In what was originally scripted as a much shorter scene, I went off into a lunatic-to-the-marvelous musical riff-rap that ended up being what's in the film today.

Scorsese let me play and DiCaprio teed me up. And that chest-bumping hum tune? That was something I was doing *before* each take to relax and keep my rhythm—it was Leonardo's idea for me to do it *in* the scene.

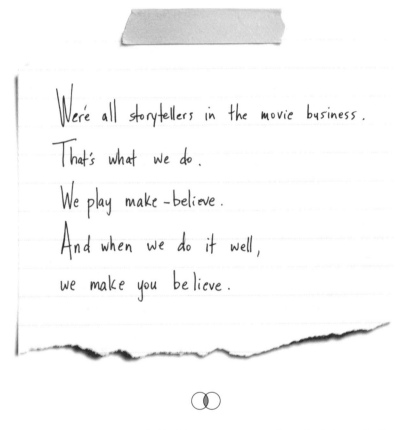

We're all storytellers in the movie business.

That's what we do.

We play make-believe.

And when we do it well,

we make you believe.

"We're shooting in the fall," I'd say to anyone who asked about *Dallas Buyers Club* and to everyone who didn't.

Like my mom, I was not asking permission.

"There is no money to make this movie, Matthew. There. Is. No. Movie," my agent said.

"Yes, there is," I said. "We're shooting in the fall."

I was not going to flinch.

I continued to lose the weight needed to tell the story properly. Now down to 150 pounds from 182, my body was getting weak but my mind was getting stronger. Every pound I physically lost seemed to be sublimating in equal amount to more mental acuity. Like Ron, I was becoming clinical, meticulous, methodical, and a perfectionist. I needed three hours less sleep a night and could drink a bottle of wine until 2:00 A.M. and still be up at four to work on the script without an alarm clock. Feverishly obsessed with *my man,* I was on fire, and I loved it. The downfall was that while my mental game was on the mound in Game 7 of the World Series, the extreme weight loss seemed to relegate my libido to the dugout.

The screenwriter, Craig Borten, had given me over ten hours of cassette recordings of Ron while he was creating and then running his alternative HIV medication Buyers Club. I listened to them constantly, picking up intonation and intention, moments of bravado and vulnerability. There was one section of recording where he and another male voice were conversing with two other women who were in the background. There was a seditiously sexual undertone in the way they talked to each other, I could tell their carnal activity with each other was recent. *But how?* I thought. Ron's got Stage 4 HIV? They couldn't be . . . Unless they *all* had HIV. Of course. How interesting, how wild, how true. I took the tape to Jean-Marc and had him listen.

"Is there any way we can get this into the movie?" I asked.

"Wow, there is something so sad and beautiful about it," he said, "but I don't know how I could touch it without it seeming ugly." Jean-Marc and I didn't speak of it again, but as you'll read, he never forgot it.

I drove to see Ron Woodroof's sister and daughter in their home in a small rural town outside of Dallas. They greeted me with open arms and complete trust as the chaperone of their brother and father's legacy. We watched old VHS tapes of Ron and the family, Ron on vacations, showing off for the camera, dressed for Halloween. They were honest about who Ron was, who he was not, and answered every question I had.

265

As we hugged goodbye, his sister asked, "Would you be interested in his diary? He kept one for years."

"If you'd allow me, I'd be honored," I said.

While the hours of tapes gave me an insight to the man from the outside in, the diary let me know who he was from the inside out. It was my secret key into Ron Woodroof's soul. The diary told me who Ron was on lonely nights; it was where he shared his dreams and fears with no one but himself, and now me. His diary is how I found *him,* who he was *after* contracting HIV, but even more important who he was *before.* I remember a guy who would lie in bed on a weeknight smoking a joint, drawing doodles in a spiral notebook, writing things like,

> *"Hope I get that call back tomorrow to go install those two JVC home speakers at Tom and Betty Wickman's house. They live across town about 42 miles away so I figure $8 gas there and back, $6 for the monster cable speaker wire I gotta supply, that'll clear me $24 off the $38 I'm charging 'em to install the speakers. Hot damn! I'll hit the Sonic afterwards and get me a double cheeseburger and a taste of Nancy."*

Then he'd wake up early the next morning, iron his one pair of slacks, his short-sleeve button-down, and put a fresh AA battery in his pager while he sipped his second cup of coffee, preparing to make a $24 profit out of his day. Until his pager buzzed, Tom and Betty's number.

"We're gonna cancel the speaker install today, found a company that costs a little more than you but they'll insure their work, thanks, Ron." His heart would sink.

"Goddamnit," he wrote.

Then he'd get high and head to that Sonic in spite of it all. Buy a single instead of a double and flirt up Nancy Blankenship, who he thought was pretty cute, especially how she roller-skated out to his car door with his food order and smiled her one-brown-tooth smile.

"She's my lucky 16," he wrote.

Come to find out, "16" was the room number of the nearest two-star motel where he and Nancy Blankenship would shag from time to time. That's why she was *lucky*.

Ron invented things but wouldn't follow up on a patent. He made plans but they never quite happened. He was a dreamer, and he couldn't catch a break.

Meanwhile, Jean-Marc Vallée and the producers continued to cast and crew the film and scouted locations in New Orleans. They did not ask permission. They did not flinch. Still, it *does* take money to make a movie, and we were running out of time on our bluff. Except we weren't bluffing, and I was still losing weight.

"We're shooting in New Orleans in the fall! The start date is October first!" we declared again more loudly to anyone who asked and everyone who didn't.

Finally someone believed us, or, believed *in* us, because that someone put up $4.9 million to finance the movie. It wasn't the $7 million dollars the film was budgeted for, but it was enough to get us in the game. Eight days before we were to begin principal photography in New Orleans, I got a call from Jean-Marc.

"I do not know how I am going to shoot this film for $4.9 million," he said. "The lowest possible budget to make it is seven mil but, if you will be there on day one, I will be there on day one, and we will make what we can make."

We both showed up.

"I've been thinking about that cassette recording you played me of Ron and the ladies and I have an idea," Jean-Marc said to me a couple weeks into shooting.

"In the scripted scene where Ron's business is doing well, what if you're in your next-door motel-room office and you see, in the line of people coming in to buy their HIV drugs, a girl you find attractive, and you ask your secretary if the girl has HIV.

"'Yeah, full-blown HIV,' she says back to you.

"Then we see Ron and this woman in the bathroom shower stall fucking, like, for need and survival."

"Sounds beautiful and true; you know how to not make it ugly?" I asked.

"I do," he said.

When you view the scene, you understand why he did. It's human, it's heartbreaking, and it's funny. While Ron and the woman are shagging in the shower next door, Jean-Marc cuts to the office where we *see* the secretaries and patrons *hearing* them, then looking around at each other in mild surprise with mischievous grins of hilarity and compassion. With humor Jean-Marc exposed the humanity. What he did not know how not to make ugly, he made beautiful.

We made *Dallas Buyers Club* for 4.9 million dollars in twenty-five days.
  We did not ask permission.
  We did not flinch.
  We took the hill.
  I got down to 135.

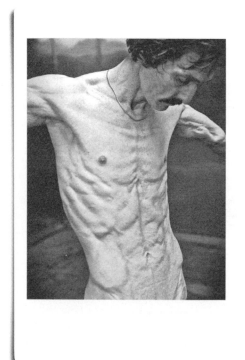

GREENLIGHT.

LIVE YOUR LEGACY NOW

"WHY ISN'T MOMMA A McCONAUGHEY?" my inquisitive three-year-old son, Levi, asked me one day.

"What do you mean?" I asked.

"I'm Levi McConaughey, Vida's Vida McConaughey, but Momma is Camila Alves. Why doesn't she have our last name?"

I thought for a second.

"Because we're not married yet."

"Why not?" he asked.

If you're a parent, then you know there are questions our children ask us that, as soon as the words come out of their mouth, we *know* we better have a great answer, because what we say next is going to be branded in their memories for life. This was one of those times.

"Good question . . . I do *want* to marry Momma. I just don't feel the *need* to. If I marry Momma, I wanna feel like I *need* to. I don't wanna do it because *that's what we're supposed to do,* or because I merely *want* to, I wanna do it when *that's what I need to do.*"

"Are you afraid to?" he asked.

273

Another one of *those* questions. I was on the stand. Apparently my three-year-old son inherited my debating skills and cross-examination capabilities. I thought again.

"Yeah, I guess I am a little bit."

"Afraid of what?"

" . . . Of losing myself," I said.

The next day I went to my pastor.

We talked about the sacrament of marriage and getting beyond my fears. He talked to me about the mystery of marriage, and how when two people who are meant to be together unite, the adventure of livin side by side does not steal the individual's sense of self, rather it enlightens and informs it. How, when two people come together to marry, they each arrive as one whole being, and in marriage we don't *lose* half of ourselves, we become *more* of ourselves. Through this covenant with God and our spouse we actually triple our existence and become three times what we were. Three entities: wife, husband, *and* God, in unification, unanimous. 1 x 1 = 3. A mystical multiplication.

"It takes courage and sacrifice," he said.

Then he challenged me. "What's the bigger risk for you, Matthew? Going on *this* adventure or continuing the one you're on?"

The dare. It got me thinking. I spent the next few weeks talking to my pastor, my brother, and successfully married men about it. Soon, for the first time in my life, I got the courage to look at marriage not as a final destination, rather as a new expedition, an affirmative and heartfelt choice to become more, together, with the woman I *wanted* to spend the rest of my life with, and the only mother I wanted to be rocking with on my eighty-eighth birthday. For the first time, I began seeing marriage as more than only a biblical and legislative sanction that I was *supposed* to feel responsible for enacting. Marrying Camila became something I *needed* to do.

I bent my knee and proposed to her on Jesus's birthday, 2011.
She said yes.
But we didn't set a date for the ceremony.

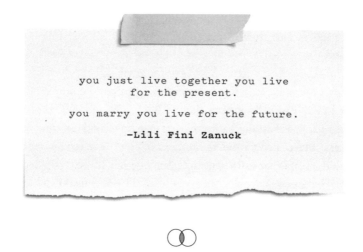

you just live together you live
for the present.

you marry you live for the future.

-Lili Fini Zanuck

Camila might have seemed totally unlike my mom, but in May 2012, five months after I proposed, she did to me exactly what my mom had done to my dad, just with an extra bonus. She handed me an invitation to my own wedding.

"Sure," I said, "all I need is a date."

Then she handed me another ultrasound.

"I have our third child growing in my belly, hon, and I'm not walking the aisle on my wedding day with a bump showing."

We invited eighty-eight of our closest friends and family. We put forty-four tents in the yard to hold those eighty-eight friends captive for an entire three-day wedding weekend, and less than a month later, on June 13, 2012, Camila Araujo Alves became Camila Alves McConaughey.

Brother Christian from the monastery presided over the Catholic ceremony, our local pastor Dave Haney did the introductory salutations, John Mellencamp played the Psalms, and a Candomblé priestess blessed us in African-Brazilian magic.

My brother Rooster said to me after the wedding, "Little brother, if there *is* a heaven, I think you got it covered."

That night at the altar Camila looked me in the eyes and said, "I don't want nothing, just *all* you got to give."

Me, I didn't marry the woman of my dreams that night, I married the best one on Earth for me, and she's a mermaid.

Afraid no more and in pursuit of a new mystery, I committed to the commitment, and for the first time in my life felt I could tumble and not fall. I knew it would be harder because now, as husband and wife, there was more to work *for*. No longer chasing butterflies, Camila and I planted our garden so they could come to us.

My mother could finally put away the Wite-Out. And Levi had one less question.

GREENLIGHT.

I'd met two men named Livingston in my lifetime. Both were men that I first noticed from a distance, similar to seeing Camila in the club that night. They were *impressions*. Both were upright, strong, and sturdy men who carried themselves with honor, constitution, and a manner of earned aristocracy. Lumberjacks by day, conductors of the philharmonic by night. Real Renaissance men, well versed in *the art of livin*. I got to know these two men quite well over time and upon closer inspection, the two of them turned out to be the very definition of my first impression.

I wanted to meet a third.

So, at 7:43 A.M., December 28, 2012, **Livingston** Alves McConaughey was born.

GREENLIGHT.

I was as fulfilled in my life as I'd ever been. Married, with three children like my father, I was finding inspiration everywhere, but now in truths, not ideas. Unimpressed with my success, I was involved in it, wanting what I needed and needing what I wanted. The more successful I became, the more sober I got; I liked my company so much I didn't want to interrupt it.

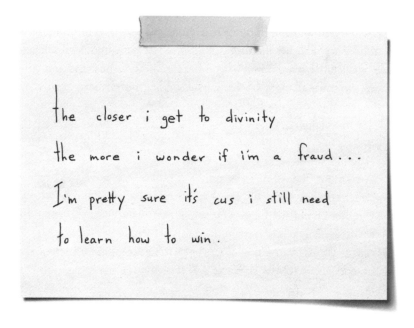

the closer i get to divinity
the more i wonder if i'm a fraud...
I'm pretty sure it's cus i still need
to learn how to win.

I received an offer for a lead role in an eight-part limited series for HBO called *True Detective*. The script by Nic Pizzolatto was so white-hot on the page I could feel the blood come off it. The fact that it was on the small screen didn't make me hesitate because the story and characters had such clear and original identities. The role I was offered was that of Marty Hart. The role I wanted was Rustin Cohle, the greatest detective I'd ever met. I couldn't wait to turn the page to see what came out of his mouth next. An island of a man who lived between the mortal respect of death and the immortal need for its deliverance. A man who, without sentiment, fiercely sought the truth no matter how much it burned. He made me sweat in *my* boots.

"If I can be Rustin Cohle, I'm in," I told them.

After a couple of days of mulling over my notion, Nic; the director, Cary Joji Fukunaga; and the producers agreed to give me Mr. Rustin Cohle. My great friend Woody Harrelson came aboard to play Marty Hart. Thankfully, he hadn't played any characters that bred copycat killers since the last time.

My family and I soon packed up and moved back to New Orleans for the six-month shoot.

I've always had a soft spot for the Crescent City. Maybe because my dad was raised there and my family visited his mom and her sisters for the Blessing of the Fleets Shrimp Festival every year growing up. Maybe because I'd also filmed four of my last five movies there. Maybe because if you want to know if you're in the good part of town or the bad, the locals' rhythmic rationale will tell you,

> *"Well, sir, there's a little bad in the good parts,*
> *and a little good in the bad parts."*

It's always felt like home.

Places are like people. They each have a particular identity. In all my travels around the globe I've written in my journal about the culture of a place, its identity. If a place and a people move me, I'll write them a love letter. New Orleans is one of those places.

Dear New Orleans,

What a big, beautiful mess you are. A giant flashing
yellow light—proceed with caution, but proceed.
    Not overly ambitious, you have a strong identity,
and don't look outside yourself for intrigue, evolution,
or monikers of progress. Proud of who you are, you know
your flavor, it's your very own, and if people want to
come taste it, you welcome them without solicitation.
    Your hours trickle by, Tuesdays and Saturdays more
similar than anywhere else. Your seasons slide into one
another. You're the *Big Easy* . . . home of the shortest
hangover on the planet, where a libation greets you on a
Monday morning with the same smile as it did on Saturday
night.
    Home of the *front* porch, not the *back*. This
engineering feat provides so much of your sense of
community and fellowship as you relax *facing* the street
and your neighbors across it. Rather than retreating
into the seclusion of the *backyard*, you engage with the
goings-on of the world around you, on your *front* porch.
Private properties hospitably trespass on each other
and lend across borders where a 9:00 A.M. alarm clock is
church bells, sirens, and a slow-moving eight-buck-an-
hour carpenter nailing a windowpane two doors down.
    You don't sweat details or misdemeanors, and since
everybody's getting away with something anyway, the rest
just wanna be on the winning side. And if you can swing
the swindle, good for you, because you love to gamble
and rules are made to be broken, so don't preach about
them, abide. Peddlin worship and litigation, where else
do the dead rest eye to eye with the livin?
    You're a right-brain city. Don't show up wearing
your morals on your sleeve 'less you wanna get your arm
burned. The humidity suppresses most reason so if you're
crossing a one-way street, it's best to look both ways.
    Mother Nature rules, the natural law capital "Q"
Queen reigns supreme, a science to the animals, an
overbearing and inconsiderate bitch to us bipeds. But
you forgive her, and quickly, cus you know any disdain
with her wrath will reap more: bad luck, voodoo, karma.
So you roll with it, meander rather, slowly forward,
takin it all in stride, never sweating the details. Your
art is *in* your overgrowth. Mother Nature wears the crown
around here, her royalty rules, and unlike in England,
she has both influence and power.
    You don't use vacuum cleaners, no, you use brooms
and rakes to manicure. Where it falls is where it lays,
the swerve around the pothole, the duck beneath the
branch, the poverty and the murder rate, all of it,
just how it is and how it turned out. Like a gumbo, your
medley's in the mix.

-June 7, 2013, New Orleans, La.

When *True Detective* aired, Camila and I watched it every Sunday night like everyone else. I obviously had the opportunity to see it all in one sitting prior to its release, but I chose to digest it as it was designed to be consumed: one hour every Sunday night, followed by watercooler talk on Monday morning, with anticipation for the next episode. It was my favorite thing on TV. Still is.

At the same time it was televised, I was on the road campaigning for awards season with *Dallas Buyers Club*. Looking back, I see that in many ways my role and work in *True Detective* was an MVP of my run for Best Actor in *Dallas Buyers Club*. It was a weekly crusade for me, the best advertisement money couldn't buy. There I was, in your living rooms every Sunday night as Rustin Cohle, then the next day in your face as Ron Woodroof on the campaign trail.

The Critics' Choice, Golden Globes, Independent Spirit, and Screen Actors Guild all presented me with the Best Actor award for my performance as Ron Woodroof. Next up was the final ceremony of the year, the Academy Awards.

I didn't have a speech planned because I believed that truly would be *bad karma*, but I did have a short list of what I wanted to talk about *if* in fact the Academy *did* call my name.

what i need
what im thankful for
whos my hero

They called my name.

I won the Oscar for Best Actor.

I was extremely honored to receive this award representing the pinnacle of excellence in my profession. It was also validation that my choices as an actor were translating as a highly competent craft. I was not half-assin it.

GREENLIGHT.

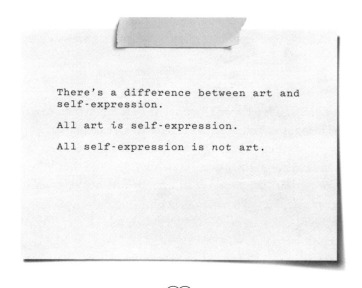

There's a difference between art and self-expression.

All art *is* self-expression.

All self-expression is *not* art.

I went on to make *Interstellar* with Chris Nolan, *The Sea of Trees* with Gus Van Sant, *Free State of Jones* with Gary Ross, *Gold* with Stephen Gaghan, *White Boy Rick* with Yann Demange, *Serenity* with Steven Knight, *The Beach Bum* with Harmony Korine, and *The Gentlemen* with Guy Ritchie. I also made a few movies for my kids, *Kubo and the Two*

Strings with Travis Knight, and *Sing* and *Sing 2* with Garth Jennings. I also became a successful car salesman as brand ambassador for Lincoln Motor Company as well as becoming the creative director for Wild Turkey bourbon.

All, characters and creations I wanted to investigate, inhabit, and become.

All, stories I found fascinating, original, and worth telling.

All, experiences I would not trade.

But, very few box office successes. Something *was not* translating. I was inviting the public but there were empty seats in the theater.

Was it me? The subject matter? The films themselves? The distributors? Bad luck? Changing times?

I don't know for sure. Little of each and more of some, I suppose.

The box office failures didn't dampen my love of acting. If anything they made me more feverishly committed to my craft. I loved performing. I loved creating. I loved getting lost in a character, then found. I loved going so deep as to see my man from the inside out. I loved the *work,* the process, the construction, the architecture of building and owning *my man.* I loved having a wife who never interrupted my belief that each role I played was the only, and last, role I'd *ever* play. I loved acting more than ever.

So much so, I began to notice that the characters and films I was doing were feeling *more* vital than who I was and the *story that was my life.* In my career now, I was more than an entertainer, I was an actor, an artist. And that satisfied me. My career was full. Wild. Dangerous. Essential. Consequential. Lively. I laughed louder, cried harder, loved bigger, loathed deeper, and felt more in the characters I was playing in the movies than the man I was livin in my life.

I said to myself, *You flipped the script, McConaughey, tipped the scale to the other side.*

282

Why pray?

A time to take inventory.

To take a look from high and wide at our
self, our loved ones, our mortality.

A time to smile upon our blessings,

to humble our selfish yearnings,

to embrace those we know are in need with
our compassion,

and see them in our mind's eye as their most
true selves,

a snapshot, down memory lane,

of those we know and care for,

when they were most themselves.

Not happiest or proudest,

not saddest or most reflective,

but that image of them when we see, without
advertisement or desire,

their light shine within,

and finally see ourselves the same,

before we say amen.

When we are who we are, and no one else.

I was *more* alive in my movies than in my life.

The stories in my profession seemed *more* vibrant than the story I was livin.

Impressions in the mirror.

Time to make a change.

So I made a plan.

Time to get rid of the filters. Make my life my favorite movie. Live my favorite character. Write my own script. Direct my own story. Be my biography. Make my own documentary, on me. Nonfiction. Live, not recorded. Time to **catch that hero I've been chasing**, see if the sun will melt the wax that holds my wings or if the heat is just a mirage. Live my legacy now. Quit acting like me. Be me.

So I gathered thirty-five years of my writings on the last fifty and took them to desolate places to seek their prudence, hear their story, and take inventory on my investment: me.

I spent two weeks alone in the desert where I was conceived, two more on the river where I learned to swim, another two in a cabin nestled in the piney woods of East Texas, three more in a motel room on the Mexican border, and two more locked up in a New York City apartment.

In each place I looked myself in the eye. All fifty years of me. It was a scary proposition. Alone with the one person responsible for *all* of it. The one person I can't get rid of. I wasn't sure I'd like what I saw. I knew it could get bloody.

And it did.

I laughed. I cried. I wrestled. I wowed.

I also had the *best* time with the *best* company I've ever had in my life.

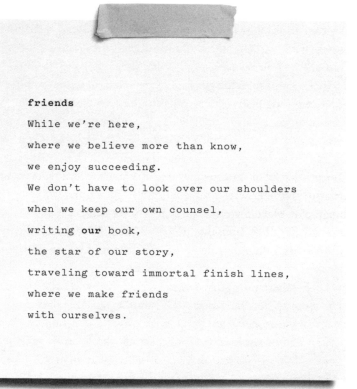

friends
While we're here,
where we believe more than know,
we enjoy succeeding.
We don't have to look over our shoulders
when we keep our own counsel,
writing **our** book,
the star of our story,
traveling toward immortal finish lines,
where we make friends
with ourselves.

So, here I am, fifty years in, looking back to look forward.

What's it all about? What's my thesis? My coda? My summation? My final remarks? What have I learned? What do I know?

As an armchair anthropologist, folk philosopher, and truth-seeking street poet, I've followed celestial suggestions, made associations, heard many voices, and dealt with reality by literally chasing down my dreams.

I have rented, had flings, hobbies, affairs, and chased butterflies to who knows where, all stops, no stays on my résumé's road to where I am today. I have found possessions, laws, relationships, careers, a wife and family, and dropped nonnegotiable anchors when I did. When I watered *their* gardens, they sprang to life, and learned lessons went from planning to performance, from *knowing* to *doing,* from acting to being. That's when the butterflies started coming to my garden.

I wrote this book so I could have a written record to hold myself accountable to. I wrote this book so *you* can hold me to task and remind me of what I forget. I circled back to prior times; lessons learned, repeated, and revisited. I noticed that the realizations arrived quickly, the learning took time, and the livin was the hardest part. **I found myself right where I left me.**

My first twenty years were where I learned the value of values. Through discipline and deep affection, I learned respect, accountability, creativity, courage, perseverance, fairness, service, good humor, and a spirit of adventure in ways that some people might consider abusive, but I remember as tough love, and I wouldn't give back one ass whupping I ever got for the value of the values my parents impressed upon me. I thank them for that.

My twenties and thirties were contradictory decades, years when I eliminated conditions and truths that went against my grain. The value in this conservative era was that it safeguarded me from fatal character debits early in life. It was a time when I was often more concerned with *not* running red lights than I was with investing in the greenlights. I did what I wanted, I learned to live. **I survived.**

My forties were a much more affirming decade, years when I started to play offense with truths I had learned and put them into action. An era where I doubled down on what fed me. The value of this liberal age was that it illuminated my most life-endorsing character assets. It was a time when I not only cruised through more greenlights because I had eliminated more red and yellow ones, but a time when I created more greenlights to travel through. A time when past reds and yellows finally turned green, as old hardships revealed themselves as good fortune, a time when the greenlights beamed brighter because I gave them more power to shine. I did what I needed, I lived to learn. **I thrived.**

As I approach the next chapter of truths to cross, the only thing I know for sure is that I will recalibrate again, and that my family will be at the core when I do. As a father, I often contradict myself, and I know I could do a better job of practicing what I preach, but I've also learned that if the message is true, don't forget it, and forgive the messenger, even if he does.

I hope to give my children the opportunity to find what they love to do, work to be great at it, pursue it, and do it. Rather than cover their eyes from ugly truths, I want to cover their eyes from fictional fantasies that will handicap their ability to negotiate tomorrow's reality. I believe they can handle it.

It's hard to find constants, natural laws, universal truths in life, but when we have kids, there is no intellectual discussion or philosophy as to how or how much to love, protect, and guide them, it's an instinctual commitment, an immediate, infinite, and ever-growing responsibility. A privilege. A greenlight.

When I was putting the finishing touches on this book earlier this year, my life, like yours, was intercepted by a red-light drama called COVID-19. Its disruption in our lives became **inevitable.** We had to stay at home, social distance, and wear masks for protection. We couldn't go to work, we lost jobs and loved ones, and we never truly knew when it would end. We were scared, we were angry. Each of us had to make sacrifices, pivot, persist, and deal—we had to get **relative.**

The tumultuous start to 2020 continued when another red-light drama introduced itself, in the name of the George Floyd murder. Its disruption in our lives soon became **inevitable** as well. There were protests, looting, riots, fear, and outrage. The unjust murder sparked a social justice revolution in America and around the world, and as racism reared its ugly head into the spotlight once again, we were reminded that All Lives couldn't matter until Black Lives matter more.

Each of us had to make sacrifices, pivot, persist, and deal—we had to get **relative.**

Both of these red lights forced us inward, literally quarantined us to search our souls for a better way forward. In doing so, we took inventory of our lives and who we are in them—what we care about, what our priorities are, what matters. We got to know our children, families, and ourselves better. We read, we wrote, we prayed, we cried, we listened, we screamed, we spoke out, we marched, we helped others in need. But how much did we change for good—its sake *and* forever?

For those of us who survived, when and how we see the benefits of what we went through during those turbulent times is **relative.** But if we work individually to make the justified changes for a more value-driven and righteous tomorrow, the red-light year that 2020 was will one day, in the rearview mirror of life, **inevitably** turn green, and per-haps be seen as one of our finest hours.

With reverence for the values my parents preached and a lifetime of traveling the world, I value culture and a culture of values. I also believe in the value of doing something well. Convinced that the best road for ourselves and society lives on the path that leads to having more **values** and **competence,** I assumed the position of Minister of Culture/M.O.C. last year, working to preserve and promote a *culture of competence and shared values* across cities, institutions, universities, academics, and athletics. Bipartisan and nondenominational, values are not only guiding principles we can all agree on, they are the fundamen-tal ethics that bring people together. When we are competent at our values *and* place more value on competence, we create a more valuable society—and that means more return on our investment, us.

Which brings me back to the other reason I wrote this book. I hope it can be useful and lend a hand if you need it, that it might teach you something, inspire you, make you laugh, remind you, help you forget, and arm you with some life tools to better march forward as more of yourself. Me? I haven't made all A's in the art of livin, but I give a damn, and I'll take an experienced C over an ignorant A any day.

I've always believed that the science of satisfaction is about learning when, and how, to get a handle on the challenges we face in life. When you can design your own weather, blow in the breeze. When you're stuck in the storm, pray for luck and make the best of it. We all have scars, we'll get more. So rather than struggle against time and waste it, let's dance *with* time and redeem it, because we don't live longer when we try not to die, we live longer when we're too busy livin.

As I've navigated the weather in my own life, getting relative with the inevitable has been a key to my success.

Relatively, we are livin. Life is our résumé. It is our story to tell, and the choices we make write the chapters. Can we live in a way where we look forward to looking back?

Inevitably, we are going to die. Our eulogy, our story, will be told by others and forever introduce us when we are gone.

The Soul Objective. Begin with the end in mind.

What's your story?

This is mine so far.

GREENLIGHTS.

Here's to catching more of them.

just keep livin,

MATTHEW McCONAUGHEY

p.s.

9-1-92

10 GOALS IN LIFE

1) become a father
2) find and keep the woman for me
3) keep my relationship with God
4) chase my best self
5) be an egotistical utilitarian
6) take more risks
7) stay close to mom and family
8) win an Oscar for best actor
9) look back and enjoy the view
10) just keep livin

While writing this book, I found this in a pile of my journal–buck slip–napkin–beer coaster notes and scribbles. I'd never seen it since I'd written it. Notice the date. Two days after finishing my first-ever acting role as "Wooderson" in *Dazed and Confused*. Fourteen days after my dad moved on. (Like I said, I guess I remembered more than I forgot.)

Acknowledgments

Thanks to my parents and brothers for giving me family, my wife and kids for creating my own, and the countless characters, inspirations, and ideals I've met along my way so far. Thanks to my heroes, from Pat to Mellencamp to me in ten years, and to all the people who gave me poems I wrote that I forgot I did.

To my friends like Seth Robbins Bindler for the courage to trailblaze, Australia for the loneliness, Don Phillips for the sight, Richard Linklater for the seen, Cole Hauser for the individuality, Gus for the loyalty, Kevin Morris for the absolute, Mark Gustawes for the belief, Mark Norby for the simplicity, John Chaney for the steady hand, Nicole Perez-Krueger for the right one, Blaine Lourd for the extra zeros, Ms. Hud for the commitment, Issa Ballo for the guidance, Mali for the home, Brother Christian for the humanity, Penny Allen for the ferocity, Pastor Dave for the context, Jordan Peterson for the clarity, Chad Mountain for the ear, Dan Buettner for the adventures, Roy Spence for the purpose, Nic Pizzolatto for the honesty, Al Cohol for the ideas, Liz Lambert for the desert, Bart Knaggs for the Llano River, David Drake, Gillian Blake, and Matt Inman for the edits, and to the WME, Crown/Penguin Random House, and Headline teams for helping me share my story on the page.

About the Author

Matthew McConaughey is the son of twice-divorced, thrice-married Jim and Kay McConaughey, married, and the father of three children. A self-proclaimed fortunate man, he considers himself a storyteller by occupation, writes poetry, and is a frustrated musician (but hey, there's still time). He is an excellent companion on a road trip, believes it's okay to have a beer on the way to the temple, and is better with a day's sweat on him. A very intentional man, Matthew feels at home in the world, likes to compare before contrasting, and is constantly seeking the common denominators in life. A crooner, a talented whistler, a wrestler, a prescriptive etymologist, and a world traveler, he believes scars are the original tattoos, and has naturally grown more hair at age fifty than he had at thirty-five. He has won six water-drinking competitions worldwide, says his prayers before meals because it makes the food taste better, is a great nickname giver, studies gastronomy and architecture, loves cheeseburgers and dill pickles, has been learning to say "I'm sorry," and enjoys a good cry once a week at church. He doesn't stop to watch his own movies if he crosses one on TV, he likes to pull things off just to see if he can, never goes to bed holding a grudge, and has recently learned there is more than one way to be right. He would rather be a sailor than an astronaut, has fluid legs on the dance floor, will take a belief over a conclusion, and believes that to all good men nontyrants, each to his own.

In 2009, Matthew and his wife, Camila, founded the j.k. livin Foundation after-school curriculum, which helps at-risk kids in over fifty-two Title 1 high schools across the nation make healthier mind, body, and spirit choices. In 2019, as well as writing this book, McConaughey became a professor of practice at the University of Texas at Austin, his alma mater, where he teaches the class he created, Script to Screen. As well as being an owner of the MLS team Austin FC, he is also the Minister of Culture/M.O.C. for the University of Texas and the City of Austin, another role and title he created. He continues to be brand ambassador to the Lincoln Motor Company and creative director for Wild Turkey bourbon, where he co-created his favorite bourbon on the planet, called Longbranch. Matthew prefers sunsets to sunrises.

jklivinfoundation.org
greenlights.com
Instagram: @officiallymcconaughey
Twitter: @McConaughey
Facebook.com/MatthewMcConaughey

Ft. Davis, Tx. May 8, 2019
    Day 4 writing "   "

dRAW blood.

i came here alone to write.

i knew blood would be drawn.

it was.

my heart pumped more through my veins than ever before.